Instructor's Manual for Strategic Marketing Cases in Emerging Markets

Atanu Adhikari • Sanjit Kumar Roy
Editors

Instructor's Manual for Strategic Marketing Cases in Emerging Markets

A Companion Volume

Editors
Atanu Adhikari
Department of Marketing
Indian Institute of Management
 Kozhikode
Kozhikode, India

Sanjit Kumar Roy
Department of Marketing
The University of Western Australia
Perth, West Australia
Australia

ISBN 978-3-319-52696-6   ISBN 978-3-319-52697-3 (eBook)
DOI 10.1007/978-3-319-52697-3

Library of Congress Control Number: 2017936050

© Springer International Publishing AG 2017

This work is subject to copyright. All rights are reserved by the Publisher, whether the whole or part of the material is concerned, specifically the rights of translation, reprinting, reuse of illustrations, recitation, broadcasting, reproduction on microfilms or in any other physical way, and transmission or information storage and retrieval, electronic adaptation, computer software, or by similar or dissimilar methodology now known or hereafter developed.

The use of general descriptive names, registered names, trademarks, service marks, etc. in this publication does not imply, even in the absence of a specific statement, that such names are exempt from the relevant protective laws and regulations and therefore free for general use.

The publisher, the authors and the editors are safe to assume that the advice and information in this book are believed to be true and accurate at the date of publication. Neither the publisher nor the authors or the editors give a warranty, express or implied, with respect to the material contained herein or for any errors or omissions that may have been made. The publisher remains neutral with regard to jurisdictional claims in published maps and institutional affiliations.

Printed on acid-free paper

This Springer imprint is published by Springer Nature
The registered company is Springer International Publishing AG
The registered company address is: Gewerbestrasse 11, 6330 Cham, Switzerland

Preface

In response to increasing demands from marketing educators, practitioners and budding managers in business schools for high-quality strategic marketing cases on emerging markets, we published a case book titled 'Strategic Marketing Cases in Emerging Markets' (Springer, 2017). The case book is a collection of short and long cases written on different industries having varying complexity and consumer behaviour. These case studies describe unique business situation and then pose several business problems which need to be solved. The dilemmas of the protagonist in these cases are carefully built to cover unique teaching objectives that are special to emerging economies. This edited case book has contributions from lecturers and practitioners from India, the UK, Turkey, Australia and other countries.

This companion volume, an instructor's manual, for the casebook is prepared by the case authors to provide instructors an overall guide that would help them in class discussion. This is a collection of teaching notes developed around the issues covered in each case. The teaching notes are written for strategic marketing and general marketing management courses at MBA, master's programmes and corporate training programmes incorporating marketing dilemmas. Set against the backdrop of respective countries, these teaching notes provide valuable information that would help instructors to prepare their classes, schedule the time and chalk out a board plan before they start the discussion in the class. Since these teaching notes include assignment and discussion questions, it will also help the instructors to divide the task between home assignment and classroom discussion.

We hope that the casebook and this companion volume would be useful to the global audience and we welcome any feedback for further improving the book.

Kozhikode, India	Atanu Adhikari
Perth, Australia	Sanjit Kumar Roy

Introduction

This is a teaching manual supporting our case book 'Strategic Marketing Cases in Emerging Markets' (Springer, 2017). The case authors in this volume provide material for instructors to understand how the cases may be introduced in the classroom and the pedagogical elements which help the student get a good grasp on the cases. The first case on *Nestle in Mexico: The Good Food Versus The Good Life Dilemma* outlines the dilemma faced by the global company in managing shareholder expectations, stakeholder expectations and the wider implications of its actions on developing a coherent and ethical marketing and communication strategy. Students can recognise and critically evaluate the role of multinational companies in using consumption-led marketing strategies in emerging economies to drive growth. The case examines the dilemma of various stakeholders in the management of the obesity epidemic in emerging economies—a result of changing food consumption patterns and the marketing of high calorific foods.

The second case on *Tanishq: Bringing Jewellery to Daily Life* provides an apt simulation of the Indian multinational company which struggles with the challenges posed by the business environment while launching a new product that will compete in the traditional market. In the executive programmes, the discussion may also lead to business strategy and issues related to the product positioning for a new product, channel selection, pricing of the product and customer segmentation. The case is structured to achieve the objectives namely to understand (1) the challenges a branded player faces when it brings a Luxury product for daily consumption, (2) the rationale for segmentation, targeting and positioning for the new offering of Mia from Tanishq, (3) possible effects of cannibalisation of Tanishq's existing product w.r.t marketing channel, and (4) the concept of experience marketing in an emerging country.

The third case on *ABC India Limited* is structured to address important learning objectives, namely (1) how to exploit a strong market opportunity that is likely to solidify in the near future due to emerging economic opportunities in India, (2) beating the intense competition in the Indian business logistics market from unorganised fragmented sector players which has been dominant in the market, (3) differentiation and repositioning strategies in highly competitive market, and (4) calculating the cost-effectiveness of usage of Hydraulic Axle and the economic value to customers.

In addition to many issues following the M&A, the fourth case *Diageo in Turkey: The Lion's Milk vs. Global Spirits* focuses on the market analysis and related decisions surrounding the marketing of the brand portfolio: Whom to target with what brands? Whether Yeni Rakı should continue its local dominancy or is it about time for Johnnie Walker, Smirnoff and Captain Morgan grand trio to have the lead role? How can Mey Icki may position and grow in the domestic and the global spirits market?

The fifth case on *To Switch or Not To Switch: Madhu's Dilemma* meets three primary teaching objectives: (1) To demonstrate the triggers and barriers to consumer switching behaviour and discuss the importance of various factors in determining a consumer's choices of a DTH service. (2) To discuss how consumers evaluate DTH services. The role of quantitative analysis is highlighted to assess the value of all competitive offerings. (3) To demonstrate the linkages between consumers behaviour insights and formulation of marketing strategies for services.

The sixth case on *Fuxmax 4D Animation Theatre* is structured to discuss (1) how to assess the viability of a substantial investment by FunMax4D in setting up the 4D theatre, (2) how to bring out the challenges in differentiation and repositioning strategies in a highly competitive environment, (3) how to identify and evaluate several strategic alternatives for FunMax4D to come out of thecurrent position and exploit a strong market opportunity that is likely to solidify in the near future and (4) how to calculate the economic value to customers to justify the premium that the company charges. The challenge, however, is to communicate this value to customers who may not be well educated but very experienced and set in their ways.

The next case on *Managing Social Media Communications at Garanti Bank* deals with multiple issues relevant in emerging markets, namely the goals and key performance indicators of social media marketing, how to identify and critically evaluate insights on which ideas for marketing communication activities in social media can be built, how to build an operational plan for customer engagement on social media, understand the prerequisites and the difficulty of establishing both a sustainable and profitable presence in social media, how budding managers appreciate the value of digital platforms in customer relationship management and how they understand the primary drivers of interaction in social media.

Next case on *Revolution Ventures* describes how a company can contribute to the education sector given the lack of quality and affordable technical education available to the masses in the back office of this world. The trigger for protagonist was his struggle in finding an easy and free source of educational material when he wanted to take up GRE or when he wanted to have an in-depth understanding of languages like SAP or Java during his professional career. This teaching note provides lot of information to the instructor to lead the case in an effective manner.

The ninth case on *M-Pesa A Disruptive Innovation From a Developing Country, Kenya* describes the developments and success of M-Pesa. M-Pesa is the first banking app for mobile phones to be developed in the developing world. It was designed by Safaricom limited Company in Kenya The product has received global attention due to its uniqueness, innovativeness, rapid adoption and the impact it has made on a large population, mostly people who are poor (bottom of pyramid). Upon reading the case study, students should be able to define the term disruptive innovation, describe the characteristics of disruptive innovation and describe the key factors attributable to successful design, development and marketing of a new product.

The tenth case on *Irrway—A Green Personal Mobility Solution* is structured to achieve the learning objectives, namely: (1) understand how to strike a balance between short-term opportunities and long-term goals and develop ways to earn smaller yet significant revenues critical for the firm's operations, (2) help students appreciate the importance of being Market Orientated for a firm, especially when it wants to serve the B2B (industrial) market, (3) help students identify the importance of segmentation of market and positioning of a product for focused marketing effort and (4) learn how to effectively communicate the value of a B2B product to the targeted customers for the benefits and not just by the product specification.

The last case on *Citrus Venture—Distressed Asset Specialist* deals with as company acquired two distressed assets (both in real estate) in Bangalore and intended to complete the development, market the product and exit the projects at a profit. One of the projects was a residential project located off Sarjapur Road. The project involved development of 65 'row houses' (which are villas connected to adjacent units by a common wall), marketing the unsold inventory and handing over the units to the end user. The case focuses on learning objectives, namely market segmentation and selection, demand and supply assessment, value offering and branding, satisfaction of various stakeholders, marketing strategy and marketing channels.

Contents

**Teaching Note: Case 1: Nestlé in Mexico: The Good Food Versus
The Good Life Dilemma**.................................... 1
Cristina Galalae and Suresh George

Teaching Note: Case 2: Tanishq: Bringing Jewellery to Daily Life..... 7
Atanu Adhikari, Ramesh Kumar Sankaran, and Trupti Karkhanis

Teaching Note: Case 3: ABC Limited........................... 17
Anshuman Sinha, Smita Das, Sumanth Naidu, and Atanu Adhikari

**Teaching Note: Case 4: Diageo in Turkey: The Lion's
Milk Versus Global Spirits**.................................... 27
Deniz Tuncalp and Selcen Ozturkcan

**Teaching Note: Case 5: To Switch or Not to Switch—Madhu's
Dilemma**.. 35
Shashi Shekhar Mishra and Arijit Pathak

Teaching Note: Case 6: Funmax 4D Animation Theatre............. 45
Rashmi Malik, Kalpit Shah, Brahmeswarar Yerrabolu,
Harikumar B. Varrier, Sumit Bhat, and Atanu Adhikari

**Teaching Note: Case 7: Managing Social Media Communications
at Garanti Bank**... 53
Kaan Varnali, Evrim Ersoy, Sezin Gul Tanriverdi, and Elif Terzi

**Teaching Note: Case 8: Revolution Ventures—Introduction
to the Service Organization and Situation Description**............... 61
Gautam Roy and Atanu Adhikari

**Teaching Note: Case 9: M-PESA: A Renowned Disruptive
Innovation from Kenya**....................................... 75
Isaac K. Ngugi and Lilian W. Komo

**Teaching Note: Case 10: Irrway—A Green Personal
Mobility Solution** 79
M.S. Chandrashekar, Gaurav Sharma, Basant P. Rangadhol,
Ashwin Petkar, Mohan Mookan, and Atanu Adhikari

**Teaching Note: Case 11: Citrus Ventures—Distressed
Asset Specialist** 85
Harsha C. Shastry, B.T. Lakshmipathi, Manohar, M.G. Srenath Rau,
Pankaj Kumar Jatarya, Sachin M. Kamtikar, and Atanu Adhikari

Teaching Note: Case 1: Nestlé in Mexico: The Good Food Versus The Good Life Dilemma

Cristina Galalae and Suresh George

Case Synopsis

Nestlé, the largest food company in the world, built on the slogan "good food for good life", has been under scrutiny especially in emerging markets for presumably utilising unethical marketing strategies. In 2014, Nestlé was fined in Mexico for promoting heavily calorific products during TV programs targeted at children. In contrast, Nestlé is the main sponsor for various interventions aiming to reduce the obesity epidemic in Mexico. For instance, Nestlé is the main sponsor of "Unidos por Niños Saludables" (United for Healthy Children), a national information campaign initiated by the Mexican Health Department, which seeks to educate parents about better diets for their offspring.

Seventy percent of the entire population and a third of the children in Mexico are obese or overweight, thus making Mexico the country with the world's highest obesity rate. Various actors with different strategic objectives are joining forces to fight obesity, in particular its infantile form. The Mexican Government introduced a junk food and fizzy drink tax. Food service operators, such as Nestlé, are joining various national initiatives aimed at encouraging consumers to develop healthier eating habits.

This case addresses the fine balancing act that Nestlé had to perform when managing the expectations of its stakeholders. On one hand, the company had to answer the calls addressed by its secondary stakeholders—such as non-governmental organizations and activist groups—and make addressing childhood obesity one of its main corporate communication messages. Simultaneously, Nestlé had to continue to promote sales of its high calorific products and satisfy its primary stakeholders, such as its stockholders or current consumers. This case study explores the dilemma that Nestle was confronted with when choosing how to

---

C. Galalae (✉) • S. George
Faculty of Business, Environment and Society, Coventry University, Coventry, UK
e-mail: ab9626@coventry.ac.uk; aa3262@coventry.ac.uk

answer the pressures and expectations of these distinct groups. The intricate intertwining of potentially non-overlapping goals, strategies and ethical conflicts are explored, with a focus on the company's marketing communication strategy.

Pedagogy of the Case Study

This case is written for strategic marketing and general marketing management courses at MBA, masters programs and corporate training programs incorporating marketing dilemmas. Focusing on the role of the emerging markets in driving growth for many multinational companies, the case examines the social implication of consumption driven marketing strategies in Latin America. It can therefore be used at graduate level courses in the ethical implications of strategic marketing in addition to MBA level courses. Using the central theme of Nestlé as a food major operating in the Latin American market of Mexico, the case can be used to develop problem-solving and decision-making skill sets of graduate level students. By focusing on a well-known food processing company, students are introduced to the process of making difficult decisions about complex human and corporate operational dilemmas.

Prerequisites

Students are expected to have a wider knowledge of issues in business ethics, corporate social responsibility, and dilemmas of multinational companies engaging in differentiating their offerings in emerging markets as well as the different aspects of marketing across borders.

Case Teaching Objectives

The case outlines the dilemma faced by the global company in managing shareholder expectations, stakeholder expectations and the wider implications of its actions on developing a coherent and ethical marketing and communication strategy.

Students can recognise and critically evaluate the role of multinational companies in using consumption led marketing strategies in emerging economies to drive growth.

The case examines the dilemma of various stakeholders in the management of the obesity epidemic in emerging economies—a result of changing food consumption patterns and the marketing of high calorific foods.

Suggested Teaching Approach

This case study and the accompanying discussion questions have been designed to facilitate teaching of a strategic marketing dilemma in emerging economies. The operations of Nestlé in Mexico is used as a pivot to introduce how food majors face challenges from both consumers, as well as from the regulatory aspect of government policies and decisions. The rise in obesity and a corresponding link to growing disposable income in many emerging economies is explored through several lenses. The first lens is that of a company seeking to expand its market and revenue base by exploiting a growing segment of consumers who demand processed food products. The second lens is that of the society in which the company operates and the associated cost of health, disease management and other related problems. The latter are explored using the context of obesity epidemic, a direct result of processed food consumption. The next lens is that of the role of the government and other stakeholders in increasing awareness of health issues and the regulatory mechanism by which food majors like Nestlé are being controlled. Each of these lenses is integrated into the context of changing consumer demands and expectations from companies and other market actors. Two learning approaches may be used to guide the teaching and learning process.

A. The instructor may use this case as part of teaching session incorporating a lecture and discussion of this case study. In this approach, a total of 90–120 min may be devoted to this approach. The first 60 min could be in the form of a lecture introducing the background theoretical context on ethics, marketing strategies, the global business environment, consumer demand in emerging markets and the regulatory mechanisms in emerging economies. This could then lead to a discussion on each of the questions at the end of the case study. Students may then be facilitated to lead discussions on analysing the context of each questions in the background of the theoretical knowledge provided by the lecture as well as their own background reading.
B. The second approach envisages the case study being used in a tutorial or seminar setting as an independent learning objective. In this approach a total of 30 min may be allocated. Students may be divided into groups and asked to lead discussions based on the questions at the end of the case study. The instructor can contribute by adding theoretical knowledge as appropriate.

In both approaches, the instructor may introduce the case study by providing an overview of the key learning objectives and the aspects of the case that are important to the learning approach chosen. The additional reading material provided in the case study teaching notes can be used by students to formulate their own perspectives regarding each of these discussion questions.

Suggested Discussion Questions

1. Describe how the obesity epidemic in Latin America can be attributed to the marketing strategies deployed by global food majors.
2. Why did the consumption patterns change in Mexico? Do you believe that this is a consequence of the economic progress that Mexico experienced in the last decades? Is there a linkage between economic growth in emerging economies and the increased consumption of high calorific food products?
3. Is Mexico is a challenging market for Nestlé? Analyse your response in the context of the changing regulatory environment for the production of food items. What can Nestlé do in order to retain its customers under the new market conditions, following the regulations imposed by the Mexican authorities?
4. Do you believe that companies should be legally obliged to behave in a responsible and sustainable fashion vis-à-vis their vulnerable customers? Undertake some online research and try to identify specific health related interventions initiated and implemented by food operators such as Nestlé, Cadbury, Mars, etc. Search for information regarding the results of these interventions. How would you evaluate their efficiency?

Suggested Answers for Discussion Questions

1. Students can start by examining the global obesity epidemic in the first instance by examining advanced economies. Macro-level analysis can then be introduced by comparing the rate of the epidemic in advanced economies to that of emerging economies. For a wider discussion of the obesity epidemic, students can access the World Health Organisation (WHO) database. This can lead to class discussions on multiple scenarios of the impact of the obesity epidemic across regions, countries and specific demographic segments. Trend analysis, as well as the relation to changing economic growth patterns across emerging economies can be used as a springboard to sensitise students to the business implications of marketing strategies that indirectly and directly contribute to this epidemic. Instructors can then link this further to the broader ethical implications of global food majors as they increase revenues from emerging economies.

   The Latin American context can be introduced into the discussion using data from the case showing that per capita consumption in the region is growing. Rising income and the increase in the consumption of processed food can also be brought into the context. This will then set the scene for the instructor to introduce the impact of the obesity epidemic on the region. The rise in obesity linked diseases and deaths, the higher rates of child obesity and the social cost of managing the disease can be articulated as part of the discussion. Comparative scenarios across emerging markets can be examined using indicators from the World Bank, as well as the World Health Organisation databases.

   The last context of the discussion could focus on how increased food processing has created opportunities for many global food majors. Nestlé could be used as an example of a company that has exploited the commercial advantages of the huge growth in this industrial sector. Integrated marketing strategy of Nestlé can be used to introduce the dilemma faced by companies in managing growth as well as responding to the wider corporate social responsibility agenda.

2. The size of Nestlé's operations in Mexico could be a starting point for discussion of this question. Details can be examined from this case study as well as from the Nestlé Mexico micro site. Students can be introduced to the traditional food habits of Mexico starting with the traditional food base of corn, beans and chilli pepper. A discussion on the nature of Mexico's food and agriculture statistics can start with reading from the FAO profile page on Mexico (http://www.fao.org/countryprofiles/index/en/?iso3=MEX). Various social indicators like the demographics of the population, the size of the household, rising income and the increasing purchasing power of children can be used to introduce how consumption patterns have changed in Mexico due to rising economic progress.

    A comparative analysis of other emerging economies as well as advanced economies can be examined using databases the World Health Organisation. This can serve as a discussion point to introduce the linkage between consumption of high calorific food products, the contributing factors from the social indicators and how increased marketing activities of food majors have led to the creation of new consumption patterns. Mexico can be used as a micro case to illustrate the change in consumption especially from the consumer viewpoint.

3. Discussion of this question can start with a reference to the previous questions where the obesity epidemic and change in consumption patterns across Latin America have been discussed. Students can then engage in a brief discussion on each of the key stakeholders; consumers, government and regulators, the media and activist groups. This will set the scene for introducing the regulatory environment of Mexico and how Nestlé is managing the challenges of government policies and changing consumer demand.

    The regulatory environment of Mexico should be cross-referenced to the ethical dilemma faced by food majors in producing processed food. The role of the food industry, the choices made by the consumer at the individual level and the wider role of the society in promoting or dissuading processed food consumption may be linked to the regulatory environment of Mexico. The challenges of managing each of these actors in the industry may be viewed in light of Nestlé's communication strategy across the country. The impact of regulatory government and societal pressures on Nestlé's financial performance needs to be examined in this context.

    The role of economic factors and social pressures on consumers making choices on the type of food products they consume could be another scenario to debate the customer retention strategy of Nestlé. Figure 2 in the case study can be used to examine this dilemma and possibly other scenarios set by students.

    Nestlé's response to the changing regulatory environment as indicated by Table 2 of the case study could be a starting point for a class discussion on different marketing scenarios. The instructor may want to focus on any one of

Nestlé's intervention and discuss alternative scenarios, thereby involving the whole class in debating its dilemma. This could then be extended to comparative geographic and economic regions.
4. Table 2 of the case study can represent the starting point to discuss how companies are legally obliged to respond to specific regulatory pressures. Students can commence by understanding the World Health Organisation (WHO) global targets on child nutrition. This may be linked back to individual research using online resources on how each food major like Nestlé manages their individual food products to conform to this targets. Marketing strategies of firms like Nestlé can be used to compare the corporate sustainability targets of other food major.

Using individual research from specific health related interventions, students can develop their own understanding of how companies should respond to customers preference for high calorific food products. Instructors may wish to use this research information to stimulate discussion on the wider business ethics agenda of food majors, the ethics agenda as practiced in other industries, the relationship between sustainability and corporate social responsibility to the bottom line of multinational companies, as well as the challenges each emerging economy presents to a global food major like Nestlé.

Using examples of non-governmental organisations (NGOs) and activist groups, students can be introduced to the role of these stakeholders in managing consumer demand as well as a regulating the business strategy of these large corporations.

Suggested Additional Reading

- Students can understand more about Nestlé and its operations in Mexico from the global site of Nestlé (www.Nestle.com) as well as the Mexico micro-site (https://www.nestle.com.mx/)
- The World Health Organisation (WHO) nutrition Department has developed and is maintaining some databases. This can be accessed at http://www.who.int/nutrition/databases/en/
- The food and agriculture organisation of the United Nations(FAO) maintains a Mexico specific database at http://www.fao.org/countryprofiles/index/en/?iso3=MEX. This can be used for background reading on the food and agriculture profile of Mexico.
- The OECD obesity update (http://www.oecd.org/health/Obesity-Update-2014.pdf) can be useful reading in understanding obesity and its effect on both emerging economies and the advanced economies.
- WHO's Member States have endorsed global targets for improving maternal, infant and young child nutrition and are committed to monitoring progress. The targets are vital for identifying priority areas for action and catalysing global change. These targets can be accessed on http://www.who.int/nutrition/global-target-2025/en/

Teaching Note: Case 2: Tanishq: Bringing Jewellery to Daily Life

Atanu Adhikari, Ramesh Kumar Sankaran, and Trupti Karkhanis

Synopsis

Tanishq the leading jewellery brand from Titan, a TATA group company is contemplating the introduction of Mia, the everyday wear jewellery collection focussed on the working women. This offering had its genesis from the earlier offering of 9 to 5 collection and everyday collection. Tanishq has identified that currently the choices of wearable everyday jewellery for the five million working women in India is limited and hence this gap is an opportunity to be tapped. However the challenges of attracting working women are high. Tanishq has to decide on the marketing mix for this offering that will effectively attract this sizeable segment for buying the Mia collection.

Potential Audience and Instructor's Material

The case has been developed for use in 'Marketing Management' course and is appropriate for MBA and Executive Development Programs as well as advanced undergraduate courses. The case is appropriate for the courses that deal with 'new product development' and even in the specialized modules focusing on product positioning, targeting and segmentation.

A. Adhikari (✉)
Department of Marketing, Indian Institute of Management Kozhikode, Kozhikode, India
e-mail: Atanu.Adhikari@iimk.ac.in

R.K. Sankaran
Indian Institute of Management Kozhikode, Kozhikode, India
e-mail: rameshkumars1@rediffmail.com

T. Karkhanis
Economics, Business and Management, IES MCRC, Mumbai, India
e-mail: Trupti.k@ies.edu

The case provides an apt simulation of the Indian multinational company who struggles with the challenges posed by the business environment while launching a new product that will compete in the traditional market. In the executive programs the discussion may also lead to business strategy and issues related to the product positioning for a new product, channel selection, pricing of the product and customer segmentation.

Objectives

The case is structured to achieve the following objectives.

1. To understand the challenges of branded player face when it brings a Luxury product for daily consumption.
2. Understand the rationale for segmentation, targeting and positioning for the new offering of Mia from Tanishq.
3. To understand possible effects of cannibalization of Tanishq's existing product w.r.t marketing channel.
4. Understand the concept of experience marketing in an emerging country.

Time Frame for Class Discussion

This case can be taught in one session of 75 min.

Suggested Discussion Questions

1. What is the Rationale of Mia as a sub brand? Discuss the various segmentation bases available to Tanishq
2. How can Tanishq attract the working women to buy everyday jewellery?
3. Is there a possibility of cannibalization when it comes to distribution of Mia?

Analysis

Answer to Question 1. What Is the Rationale of Mia as a Sub brand?

For Tanishq to improve market share, mind share and maintain growth, it should maintain its competitive advantages. The sources of competitive advantages Tanishq has traditionally depended on the following.

– TATA brand backing and the source of funds
– Purity of Gold used and Trust developed, introduction of Karatmeter
– Maintaining ethical practices and transparency in dealings

- Use of Technology in manufacturing
- Ability to develop and introduce new offerings/collections targeted at niche segments to serve the needs of that segment
- Wide range of innovative and unique designs, designed by the in house award winning design team
- Wide network of retail stores which was being expanded
- Better service and ambience at stores
- Customer loyalty programs
- Gold buy back options

Hence ability to systematically introduce new collection serving niche segments is an important competitive strength for Tanishq.

Discuss the Various Segmentation Bases Available to Tanishq

Tanishq is one of the most prominent jewellery brands in India who successfully challenged the traditional jewellery offering practices of the local jewellers by bringing the issue of rampant purity issues in the gold jewellery offered by them. By bringing in the use of Karat meter in their stores to check the purity of gold in their offerings they successfully promoted trust as the important promise in their gold jewellery. By offering a large range of designs and expanding their retail reach to 126 stores in 76 cities they were able to carve out a 5% of the total jewellery market of Rs. 1000 billion. The jewellery business of Titan now contributes to 76% of the company's revenues and has registered a CAGR of 40.45% since 2007.

The jewellery business of Titan has three brands focussed on different segments of the market. Zoya, the brand in the luxury segment focuses on the design discerning, high end customer. Tanishq brand was targeted at the progressive women and focussed on the premium and mid-market. Gold Plus was the third brand and focussed on the mass market. The company have been regularly introducing various collections of jewellery under the three brands.

Indian Jewellery Industry

The jewellery market is expected to touch Rs. 1000 billion and is predominantly dominated by local/traditional jewellers from the unorganised sector. The market share of the branded jeweller has been about 10% of this total market. The growth and acceptance of the branded jewellery has prompted some of the traditional players to increasingly focus on brand building with many of them moving from one to two shop business to multi shop at different geographical locations.

The key components of the Jewellery industry are as given below.

(a) Metal	
Gold	Yellow
	White
Silver	
Platinum	
(b) Studded Jewellery	
Diamond	
Gems	
Pearl	

Gold jewellery is the predominant one in the jewellery industry.

Segmentation at Tanishq was followed from customer driven perspective. Hence the following options are present.

1. Where consumer wears jewellery
2. Consumer purchase occasions

These two options presented the following: Wear Occasions and purchase occasions:

Wear occasions	Details
Everyday	Workplace, Home
Special occasion wear	Contemporary, Traditional
Wedding jewellery	Bridal wear, Fashion jewellery

Purchase Occasions

Purchase occasions	Details
Festivals	Diwali, Akshaya Tritiya, Karva Chauth, Varalakshmi Vrat, Dussehra, Onam, Pongal etc.
Special occasions	Birthdays, Bonus/Extra money, Fall in price of gold

Based on wear occasions Everyday wearable jewellery is an option that Tanishq had introduced earlier also (9 to 5 collection and Everyday collection). From the demand side the following factors are important indicators of the segment for women's everyday wear.

– Increase in number of working women
– Rising disposable incomes amongst working women
– Changing consumer preferences for lightweight jewellery with high design quotient
– Growing urbanisation

- Brand image and trend conscious working maidens
- Need for jewellery matching the workplace attire
- The working maidens are outward directed in personality
- Working women without children hangout more with friends

Tanishq identified that out of the estimated five million working women only less than fifty thousand shopped at Tanishq. It was also seen that though competition had jewellery for daily wear, the offerings were not focussed. The characteristics mentioned above are seen in working women from SEC A and SEC B. Hence coupled with the characteristics of the working women mentioned above there is a distinct opportunity for the daily wear offering.

It is also seen that the working wives are inner directed, less conscious of their looks and need for personal care products and are price conscious. They would be a challenging segment to draw to the offering of Mia from Tanishq. These women would be more in the age of 32 years and above. This group might not be a good segment of customer for the new offering to target.

Answer to Question 2. How Can Tanishq Attract the Working Women to Buy Everyday Jewellery?

The process of Gold Jewellery purchase is an emotional and highly involved one. Gold jewellery, on a rational basis is popular as an investment. The rise of disposable incomes and lifestyle has resulted in consumption of branded products. The number of households, by 2015 in middle class and the rich is expected to rise as shown in Exhibit 3. Consequently the disposable income is also expected to rise. The urban population is also expected to rise by 2021. This is a huge opportunity for the branded products including branded jewellery.

The five million strong working women is a distinct segment that can be focussed for the branded jewellery offering. The working maidens amongst the group of working women are the most attractive group from the segment as they are more brand image and trend conscious and tend to be outward directed in personality. They are seen relatively more in the corporate set up and are highly educated. The working mothers and wives would be the challenging group from the working women segment to attract for the offerings of branded products for jewellery and personal care products.

Traditionally gold jewellery has been purchased during special occasions like weddings, festivals and was more emotion based which would have been supported by the rational thinking of investment opportunity in gold purchase. However there is now a relative decrease in trend of gold jewellery purchase as investment option and an increase in design and style gaining importance as purchase drivers. Further for investment purchase the increasing trend is to buy gold coins/medallions as they provide better returns.

Studies also reveal that other than festivals and special occasions jewellery purchase is seen during the following occasions;

- Fall in gold prices
- When bonus and extra money is received

Hence marketers can simulate the purchase occasions more evenly through the year with well-designed marketing programs like launch of new jewellery collections, exchange programs, advertise for more occasions etc. It is also seen that the tastes of urban and rural customers vary and it is important to offer jewellery depending on the regional preference as seen from the Gold Plus offering of Titan.

The option of where to purchase gold jewellery was based on loyalty and trust developed between the jeweller and the customer. Traditionally the family jeweller would have been a local jeweller who would have been patronised by the customer for generations. The challenges the branded jeweller face is that the perception that they are more costly to increasing the mind share and share of voice. However the emphasis of purity of gold, wide range of designs and service offered has helped in increasing acceptance of branded jewellery.

Advertising and Promotion

Jewellery business of Titan indulges in TVC's, outdoor hoarding and print media advertising. Tanishq focuses on creating relevance across the space for premium and mid-market segments with its collection. For the TVC's Tanishq has been focussing on the emotional space rather than the model decked in gold theme. In print the company now focuses on show casing the width and range of collection whereas when Tanishq was launched the emphasis was on purity of the gold in its offering. BTL campaigns are also focussed on. Titan's jewellery business also runs two customer loyalty programs Anuttara and Ananta.

Answer to Question 3. Is There a Possibility of Cannibalization When It Comes to Distribution of Mia?

When Tanishq was launched the company offered its products through multi brand outlets. However as this model did not help the brand and sales they moved to their own retail stores network. Currently the retail distribution is through three different formats of Company Owned and Company Operated (COCO) stores, Franchise Owned and Franchise Stocked stores and Franchise Owned and Company stocked stores. The details of the number of stores for each of the brands are as given.

Zoya: 2 Stores, one in Delhi and one in Mumbai.
Tanishq: 120 retail stores in 76 cities.
Gold Plus: 29 stores in Tamil Nadu.

Teaching Note: Case 2: Tanishq: Bringing Jewellery to Daily Life 13

The focus of the company is now to establish large format stores of 20,000 sq. ft. area compared to the normal 2000–3000 sq. ft. area. The company has two modern manufacturing plants, one at Hosur and the other at Dehra Dun. The manufacturing unit employs advanced process of dust extraction system that reduces the gold wastage encountered during manufacturing to almost 2% which was considerably lower than what the local jeweller would be facing. The company also has a in-house design studio comprising of award winning designers who brings out unique designs that is a strength for the company.

Traditionally pricing of the gold jewellery was primarily based on the price of gold and the weight of gold used in the product. The other cost components to be considered for pricing was the making and wastage charges, the weight of gold and other gems and diamonds and government levies. The making and wastage charges would also include the margins which would be based on the design, the caratage and also the intended wear occasion. This would be taken as a percentage of the price of gold used in the jewellery. This component can vary between 12 and 14% for normal jewellery and can go up to 35% for unique designs and antique jewellery.

The collections on offer from Tanishq were affordably priced at the entry level. However they were higher than the products on offer from the unbranded segment. The branded players are moving away from pricing based on the price of gold on that day and weight of gold used in the product to fixed price for the piece of jewellery.

Suggested Assignment Question

1. What can be the value proposition for Mia?
2. What are the positioning, promotion and pricing strategies adopted by Tanishq to promote Mia?

Analysis

1. Value proposition
    The customer is contemplating to introduce Mia as a sub brand to Tanishq. This sub brand will help in tailoring the everyday jewellery wear focussed on the niche market of working women between 25 and 35 years. This would actually help in better focus compared to the earlier "9 to 5 collection" and "everyday collection". However Tanishq should focus on supporting the brand completely with promotion and budget as otherwise it would be difficult for Mia to find the right identity with the customer. Also the relevance has to be communicated well.
    As per Kulhalli during the launch of Mia, he emphasized on value of Mia and said, "The brand is meant for women on the go, who are engaged in various professions and have a well-established accessory ensemble, unfortunately

excluding jewellery. Fine jewellery that working women buy is mostly for traditional occasions, and do not have an offering for their daily wear in the market. Tanishq, the national jeweller of India, is best suited to understand the needs of these consumers and has put together a wonderfully-crafted, well-designed jewellery collection, which will make them love to go to work!"

Talking about the collection, Revathi Kant, design head, Tanishq, said, "Mia is a tribute to today's working woman. The design inspiration is derived from an in-depth understanding of her life. This collection is high on design quotient, light in weight, affordable and apt for today's modern woman."

2. Positioning

The competitive frame of reference: The target segment is the urban working women between 25 and 35 years from SEC A and SEC B. The nature of competition would be mainly on 18 Karat offerings with diamond, other gem stone studding. There could be enamel based offerings also. Price is also a basis especially in localised markets where local players could imitate the offerings.

The Point-Of-Parity
– 18 Karat gold based jewellery with or without gemstones, diamond
– Lightweight jewellery
– Offering through retail stores and possible multi brand outlets
– Similar price range compared to branded competition

The Point-of-difference
– A separate sub brand
– High on design quotient, contemporary design
– Wide range of designs
– Tanishq promise backing
– Engage the customer more. Designs selected based on focus group interactions

Product Strategy

The collection would have lightweight 18 Karat gold based jewellery with or without gem stone studding. The designs are based on the focus group interactions and inspired by geometrical shapes and floral designs.

Value-Chain Strategy

Mia being a sub brand of Tanishq should be offered through its present retail store network. To start with Tanishq should focus on the metros of Mumbai, Delhi, Bangalore, Hyderabad, Kolkata and Pune. The company also has the option of offering the Mia collection through TATA group company Trent's Westside retail chain. Westside is a large format lifestyle retail store with 53 stores of 8000–34,000 sq. ft.

Pricing Strategy

Since the branded competitors offer similar offering in the range of INR 9000 to INR. 50,000 the Mia range should also be in that range. However keeping relevance of the Tanishq positioning for Premium and Mid-market the company could charge higher for products with better design. Average price for a product with good design offering should be around INR 25,000.

Promotion Strategy
Effective combination of advertisement, sales promotion, public relations to engage the customer is important. The promotional activities done for the earlier launches like presentations to working women at several corporate offices, cross-promotional tie ups with working women spaces like music stores, beauty salons, lifestyle stores and book stores should be targeted. TVC's, outdoor hoardings, print advertisements etc. have to be done. Internet especially social networks also have to be extensively used for customer engagement. It would also be worthwhile to engage the customers for creating designs to enable more engagement and buy in for the products.

Postscript

Tanishq, launched its Mia, a line of jewellery specially made for working women. Mia has been particularly designed for today's working women who until now had not much of a choice with the formal line of jewellery. The line comprises two distinct designs directions, one in the modern and another in the ethno contemporary space; spread across modern silhouettes of earrings, finger rings, pendants, and bangles with a twist.

The design in the Mia collection incorporates fine geometry, complexity and textures. The assortment has captured floral graphics, abstraction and hint of colours through the use of mother of pearl, which is a key feature. The forms are voluminous yet very light with techniques such as electroforming and filigree casting that have helped to impart the new look. Tanishq's advertising agency, Lowe Lintas has created three new TVCs for the launch. In the three TVCs titled, 'Parking', 'Increment' and 'Workshop' a woman is shown delighted to go to work because of her new Mia jewellery, even though she has issues like parking outside her office, the increment she receives from office and the monotonous workshops she needs to sit through.

Apart from the collection itself, yet another feature that sets it apart is its online campaign. The digital strategy crafted for this very unique jewellery line is equally inspiring. Right from a very exciting start with a pre-launch micro site (http://bit.ly/WhatareYouMissing) that built the curiosity of the audience with thought-provoking videos of real working women, to a first-of-its-kind interactive video catalogue. The response to the campaign has been overwhelming with the attention of thousands of working women. The Mia line of fine jewellery has over 100 designs and is a 'dream come true' for over five million working women in India who didn't have a one-stop shop for formal jewellery wear until now. Priced at Rs. 5999 onwards, the collection is available across the 130 Tanishq outlets in over 76 towns.

Teaching Note: Case 3: ABC Limited

Anshuman Sinha, Smita Das, Sumanth Naidu, and Atanu Adhikari

Synopsis

ABC India Ltd. (ABCIL), started in 1963 was a pioneer in the field of logistics since its inception. The company was specialized in surface transportation, international freight forwarding and integrated logistics services. ABCIL got their business plunged off as they were not able to generate new business and was even facing challenges in maintaining its market share. It was feeling the heat of intense competition from both large Full Truckload FTL competitors who constantly negotiated bargains with their larger customers to wean away those accounts, and from smaller fleet owners whose lower-cost structures and scant regard for regulations allowed them to undercut prices to smaller and mid-tier customers. In order to maintain its position and market share, the company has to come up with viable and long sustaining solution.

A. Sinha (✉)
Barclays Technology Center India, Pune, India
e-mail: sinha.ans@gmail.com

S. Das
Business Consulting, NTT DATA, Hyderabad, India
e-mail: dassmita@gmail.com

S. Naidu
Infosys Ltd, Hyderabad, India
e-mail: sumanth.20.02@gmail.com

A. Adhikari
Department of Marketing, Indian Institute of Management Kozhikode, Kozhikode, India
e-mail: Atanu.Adhikari@iimk.ac.in

Case Objectives

The case is structured to achieve the following learning objectives:

1. Exploit a strong market opportunity that is likely to solidify in the near future due to emerging economic opportunities in India.
2. Beating the intense competition in the Indian business logistics market from unorganized fragmented sector players which has been dominant in the market.
3. Differentiation and repositioning strategies in highly competitive market.
4. Calculate the cost effectiveness of usage of Hydraulic Axle and the economic value to customers.

Position in Course

This case has been developed for use in marketing management as well as marketing strategy courses and is appropriate for MBA, executive development programs and advanced undergraduate courses in strategic marketing management. The case suits in courses that deal with business strategy for large and medium enterprises which showcase the importance of agility in business.

Suggested Assignment Questions

ABCIL had to address below issues in early 2010 in order to retain its customer base and continue to be the pioneer as in the past.

1. What kind of improvisation do you suggest ABCIL and in which areas to reach its objectives?
2. What unique factors with which ABCIL can differentiate itself from FTL and small fleet competitors? Should the company work towards strengthening those?
3. Can ABCIL afford competitive pricing since it has large volumes?
4. Since retaining customer base is most important, how can ABCIL achieve this and which should be a long sustainable solution?
5. How should ABCIL plan to tackle the volatility of fuel price in Indian market?

Suggested Readings

1. Basic road statistics to understand surface transportation in India:
   [Source:http://www.indiaenvironmentportal.org.in/files/file/basic%20road%20statistics%20of%20india.pdf]
2. Financial performance of ABCIL:
   [Source:http://www.careratings.com/upload/CompanyFiles/RR/ABC%20India%20Ltd-03-13-2014.pdf]

Suggested In-Class Discussion Questions

In order to engage the class and drive in the right direction, the instructor can put forward the below questions for discussion.

1. What kind of competitive threats ABCIL should consider while analyzing the current situation? Supportive content can be found at Fig. 1.
2. The class can go through Exhibit 9 in the case (also shown as Table 1) and suggest the best type of truck beneficial for long distance cargo.
3. Analyze the benefits of 3PL logistics model and suggest if further investment in this wing can help ABCIL achieve the mentioned objectives.

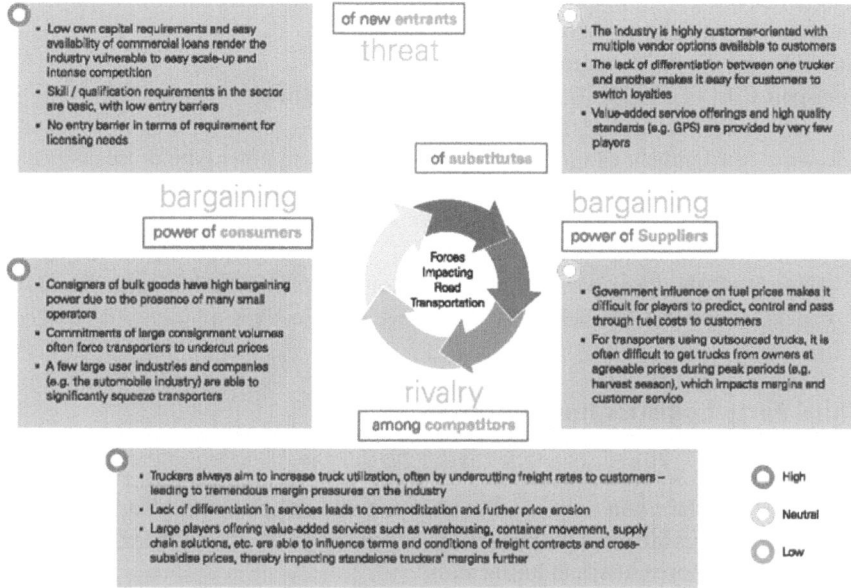

Fig. 1 A typical Market threat competitive chart affecting the logistics sector

Table 1 Cost of the carrier corresponding to type of truck

Type of truck	Laden wt. in kg	Passing wt. in kg	Sizes (LBH)	Mileage (km/l)	Cost of the carrier
6 wheeler	16,200	9000	17 × 7 × 8	7	INR 40,000.00
10 wheeler	25,200	16,000	22 × 7 × 8	7	INR 80,000.00
12 wheeler	31,000	22,000	22 × 7 × 8	7	INR 120,000.00
Normal trailer	35,200	20,000	36–40 × 8 × 8	5	INR 150,000.00
Double Axel Trailer	40,200	27,000	36–40 × 8 × 8	5	INR 180,000.00
Triple Axle Trailer	49,000	35,000	36–40 × 8 × 8	5	INR 200,000.00
Hydraulic Axle	600,000	Unlimited	ul*3 m*15 ft.	5	INR 900,000.00

Source: Created by the authors from company files

Analysis

1. Can ABCIL tackle the operating cost by the introduction of Hydraulic Axle? Consider about consignment of 5000 bikes each 105 kg that need to be transported from Mumbai to Chennai which is roughly around 1332 km. Compare the cost required for Triple Axle trailer and Hydraulic Axle.

Triple Axle Trailer:
Total passing weight = 5000 × 105 = 525,000 kg
Passing weight of one Triple Axle Trailer = 35,000
No. of Triple Axle Trailers required = 525,000/35,000 = 15
Transport Cost of one Triple Axle Trailer = INR 200,000
Transport Cost of 15 Triple Axle Trailers = 15 × 200,000 = **INR 3 Million**
Hydraulic Axle:
Total passing weight = 5000 × 105 = 525,000 kg
No. of Hydraulic Axles required = 1
Transport Cost of one Hydraulic Axle = **INR 0.9 Million**

The same consignment example can be used to compare other type of trucks listed in the exhibit with Hydraulic Axle and arrive at a decision of investment on Hydraulic Axle.

2. Analyze all the three possible improvisation approaches and suggest the most beneficial one that can help ABCIL achieve its objectives.

Third Party Logistics Improvisation

Pros
- Flexibility: Since you only pay for what you use and can walk away whenever you want, 3PLs are ideal for businesses that aren't yet ready for the commitment of leasing a warehouse and hiring staff.
- Convenience: Outsourcing your logistics leaves you to focus on other important aspects of your business. You simply send your customers' orders to your 3PL and the 3PL dispatches them for you. At the end of the billing period, you receive one consolidated invoice for the services used, which usually comprises a "rent" that is based upon the volume of space you are occupying; plus a fee for each order processed; plus a fee for freight management.
- Expertise: From simple things such as labeling and bar-coding your products through to trading electronically with larger retailers, your 3PL's experience and access to the latest technologies mean they'll be more organized and better at it than you.
- Better transport rates: As they organize deliveries for all their clients, your 3PL is in a position to get volume discounts from freight carriers, which may be passed on to you.

- Professional example: Working closely with a 3PL enables you to learn the basics of warehousing and distribution management, which can be extremely useful should you decide to setup your own warehouse in future.

Cons
- Cost: Convenience comes at a price; the overall cost of using a 3PL is far greater than if you managed your logistics yourself.
- Loss of direct control: You are relying on the competency, reliability and honesty of the 3PL and its staff, and must assume that they know what they are doing and are always acting in your best interests.
- Distance: You may be several hundred kilometers away from your warehouse and merchandise, which can be a serious problem if, for example, there are quality problems with a batch of your product. Furthermore, if you have any concerns or complaints about service, you are limited to communication by phone and email.
- Potential loss of reputation: The 3PL is responsible for one of the most critical functions of your business. Their mistakes reflect directly on you and your customer will not accept you passing the buck on to your subcontractor.

Third-party logistics providers can be very useful to the small business operator, particularly those who are just starting out. A common approach is to use a 3PL in the early stages of the business, before moving on to establish a warehouse once the additional responsibility of doing so is justified by the reduced operational costs to your business.

Warehouse Improvisation

Pros
- Control: This is the rationale behind most decisions to expand and keep warehousing in-house. The control of processes, physical inventory and data is obviously harnessed most effectively when your organization maintains its own storage and distribution facilities and workforce.
- Specialization: For some companies, warehouses require highly specialized skills and equipment to run. Even the storage facilities may need to be specially designed. Similarly, when your organization performs a number of activities which add value to products or services, keeping inventory under your own roof can be more viable than outsourcing.
- Stakeholder Confidence: Because you have direct control of in-sourced warehousing, your customers and other stakeholders know they are dealing with a single organization. This can be important when your business relies on long-term contracts or service agreements with sensitive or demanding customers.

Cons

- Increased Capital Expenditure: With in-house warehouses, your company has to bear the costs of associated property leases and warehouse manpower cum equipment. While there is of course, a cost associated with warehousing as a service, many companies find outsourcing to be a cost saver overall.
- Risk Overhead: With in-house warehousing, the whole risk associated with managing people and processes is on you. Whereas in case of out sourced warehousing, your business won't get caught out by peaks and troughs in demand, which can otherwise leave you with an under or over-utilized facility and workforce.

Realistically, the decision to in-source or outsource your warehousing should be based on extensive analysis of your own particular business and its requirements. Many businesses can benefit from warehouse outsourcing, hence its growth as a supply chain strategy. The important thing though, is to understand your operational objectives well, and apply whichever model best enables them to be met, without sacrificing any competitive advantage.

Technology Improvisation

The best improvisation approach is new cutting edge technology beyond the scope of other competitors in the segment. Through this the achievement would be more significant as the price-profit dependency matrix is higher on costs of transportation than on warehousing. Thus the company chose to concentrate on transportation technology improvisation at first. In their strive to bring their operations to world-standards, ABCIL's research led them to introduce Hydraulic axle trailers for the first time in Indian logistics market. This poised them to capture one of the major market segments in Manufacturing and Infrastructure which were set to grow even bigger owing to India's huge rate of economic and industrial growth.

Introduction of Hydraulic Axle in ABC

Hydraulic Axle Trailer is a loading platform available in different modules or configuration, having multi Axle unit connected by a hydraulic suspension. Hydraulic/Pneumatic hoses are fitted throughout the trailer to facilitate the hydraulic function from the respective tank by adjusting the different control valves as seen in Exhibit 13 in the case. ABC Logistics launched the Hydraulic Axle fleet which could have the advantages over other fleet as mentioned in the case.

What Happened

The high growth segment requires a fast, safe and technologically advanced loading-unloading system.

ABCIL decided to achieve this by introducing the hydraulic axle fleet which would be self-owned cutting the 3PL margins and making the best from the high profit segment products. It is evident that an early initiative in investing of upgrading its technology gave ABCIL the required edge over its competitors. Spurred by the growths infrastructural and manufacturing industry the need was felt for massive-load carrying transportation. By being the first adapter of hydraulic axle type trailers in Indian logistics industry, the company cut all competition and became leader in these segments.

Final Outcome

The results due to the timely decisions made by the ABC leadership are summarized below:

Experienced Promoter
ABC was initially a part of TCI-Bhoruka group, promoted by Late Mr. P. D. Agarwal, with the largest company of the group being Transport Corporation of India Ltd. Mr. A.K. Agarwal (son of Mr. P. D. Agarwal), the main promoter of ABC, has over three decades of experience in transport business. It was under his leadership that ABC has become an established mid-sized player in road transportation industry. He and his son, Mr. Ashish Agarwal (managing director), look after the day-to-day affairs of the company, with support from a qualified management team having adequate experience in the transportation business.

Satisfactory Fleet of Vehicles of Reputed Make
ABC Logistics launched the Hydraulic Axle fleet which could have the following advantages of hydraulic excel over other fleet. ABC's vehicles fleet size has increased considerably over the years. All its vehicles are of reputed make and majority of such vehicle is less than three years old, the annual maintenance of which is taken care of by the respective manufacturers. Building of large assets base is expected to benefit the company in the long run through sourcing of large size orders from reputed clients, albeit at the cost of high leveraging and capital charge. Further, low order book position in recent times has resulted in underutilization of the fleets to considerable extent impacting the profitability.

Intense Competition Leading to Pressure on Margins
A major part of transportation business in India is dominated by unorganized sector players. High fragmentation leads to unhealthy price war and discounts, resulting in depressed freight rate. However, ABC offers integrated logistics solutions using multi-modal transportation including state of the art warehousing facilities,

customized services and other value added services which has helped ABC in building its brand in the logistic industry.

Sustaining the Volatility in Fuel Price

Volatility in fuel price is an inherent factor for any logistic company. Majority of the contracts of ABC include price escalation clause, due to which the company is able to pass the fuel price hike. In case of fixed price contracts, the expected fuel price hike is embedded in the contract price itself.

Improvement in Capital Structure

ABC's capital structure has remained moderate over the last three years with long term debt- equity ratio being comfortable at below unity level as on March 31, 2013. Overall gearing ratio improved significantly as on March 31, 2013 to 1.54× as against 2.15× as on March 31, 2012 due to lower working capital borrowings in view of reduced sales and accretion of profit (arising out of above mentioned stake sale) to reserve.

Suggested Teaching Approach

In order to create curiosity and interest among the students before taking right decision, the instructor can divide the class into three different groups and assign the below mentioned possible solutions, one to each group. A debate can be conducted among the groups discussing the pros and cons of the solutions models. The possible solutions are:

- Third Party Logistics Improvisation
- Warehouse Improvisation
- Technology Improvisation

Vision for the Future

Ashish Agarwal has taken the right approach to invest in technology improvisation as road transportation is the only segment where most experts are of the opinion that development must take place rather swiftly. There is competition in the road transportation segment of the industry, where small players have mushroomed. According to certain estimates, the overall costs of the logistics industry is estimated to be 14% of India's gross domestic product (GDP), which is translated as US$141 billion if one considers India's GDP to be $1 trillion. Of the seven categories of the industry, experts feel that Multi-nodal Transport Operators will do well in the coming years as shown in Fig. 2, considering the inherent better returns due to the light asset model of the business. These operators derive returns on equity in the range of 15–20%.

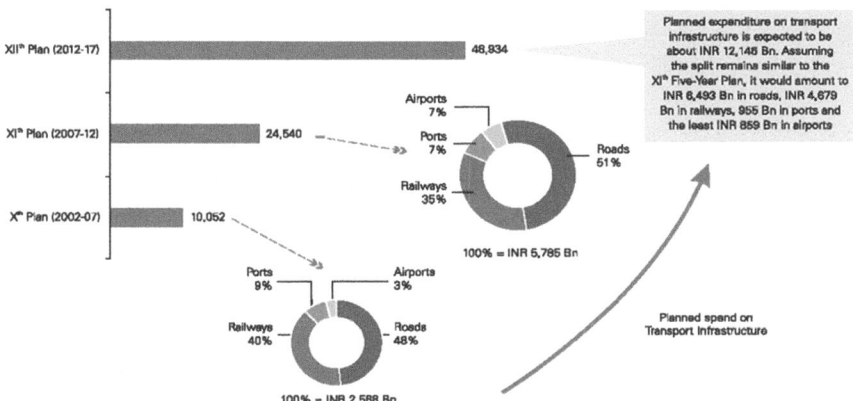

Fig. 2 Five-Year Plans—Infrastructure spend (INR Billion)

Teaching Note: Case 4: Diageo in Turkey: The Lion's Milk Versus Global Spirits

Deniz Tuncalp and Selcen Ozturkcan

Case Synopsis

Case starts with a global giant acquiring a local giant company. Both companies own some very strong brands. Post-acquisition era demands a new marketing strategy. The defined market, and the nature of competition need to be revisited. Competitive competencies need to be re-identified, in the face of changing economic, political, and taxation conditions in Turkey and abroad.

In addition to many issues following the M&A, our focus is on the market analysis and related decisions surrounding the marketing of the brand portfolio: Whom to target with what brands? Whether Yeni Rakı should continue its local dominancy or is it about time for Johnnie Walker, Smirnoff and Captain Morgan grand-trio to have the lead role? How can Mey Icki may position and grow in the domestic and the global spirits market?

The instructor should start by directing the question that the two managers are facing in the case: What should be the future direction of Mey/Diageo both in Turkey and internationally? Here some students are expected to favour continuation of the Yeni Rakı marketing investments, while others might favour Johnnie Walker, Smirnoff vodka or Captain Morgan's. This icebreaker entry would facilitate the discussion of the questions listed in the teaching note section.

D. Tuncalp (✉)
Istanbul Technical University, Istanbul, Turkey
e-mail: tuncalp@itu.edu.tr

S. Ozturkcan
Bahcesehir University, Istanbul, Turkey
e-mail: selcen.ozturkcan@comm.bau.edu.tr

Learning Outcomes

After analysing this case study, the student should be able to do the following:

1. Analyse the environment, competition, industry and product positioning.
2. Compare pre- and post-acquisition market structures and its effects on marketing strategy.
3. Analyse customers and market segmentation.
4. List alternative marketing strategies and market positioning.
5. Demonstrate expected strategy outcomes based on scenarios.

Level of Program Where the Case to Be Taught

The case is designed for MBA, executive MBA and senior undergraduate students. It can be used to teach concepts of Market Analysis, Marketing Strategy, Corporate, Business and Marketing Strategy, Strategic Market Segmentation.

Suggested Assignment Questions

1. The spirits market was growing in Turkey but slower than other emerging markets. Did Diageo made the best decision to simply enter the Turkish market with acquisition, or should it try to expand its existing operations organically in Turkey pushing its international brands?
2. A market analysis of Turkey would include a qualitative and quantitative evaluation. Based on the information in the case and other information that you can collect on the Internet, which quantitative figures would be most important for the market analysis? How would market potential and market concepts apply to your analysis?
3. As part of the environmental analysis, what environmental forces are in favour and against Diageo's acquisition or the spirits market in general in Turkey?
4. Develop a preliminary competitive/industry analysis for spirits market in Turkey. What are major advantages and weaknesses of Diageo/Mey, when compared with the competition?
5. What complications emerge from analysing the spirits market in Turkey, as compared with analysing the spirits market in your country or in the US?
6. What brand/product positioning does Yeni Rakı hold for which targets?

Suggested Readings

- Diageo to Buy Turkish Distiller Mey Icki for $2.1 Billion
  http://www.bloomberg.com/news/articles/2011-02-20/diageo-said-to-be-close-to-buying-distillery-mey-icki-of-turkey (Fletcher, 2011)

- Diageo Seeks Turkey Drink Limit Balance After Mey Icki Purchase
  http://www.bloomberg.com/news/articles/2013-05-16/diageo-seeks-turkey-drink-limit-balance-after-mey-icki-purchase (Harvey & Fletcher, 2013)
- Diageo's Turkish Unit Under Investigation by Competition Board
  http://www.bloomberg.com/news/articles/2015-08-11/diageo-s-turkish-unit-under-investigation-by-competition-board (Finkel & Buckley, 2015)
- Diageo's $2.1 Billion Turkish Hangover
  http://www.bloomberg.com/bw/articles/2013-06-24/diageos-2-dot-1-billion-turkish-hangover (Stock, 2013)
- Turkey's Liquor Market at Risk
  http://www.bloomberg.com/bw/articles/2013-06-20/turkeys-liquor-market-at-risk (Schweizer & Hacaoglu, 2013)
- Acquisition of Mey İçki
  http://tinyurl.com/hjubggo (Diageo, 2011)
- Diageo to Acquire Mey Icki Q&A
  http://tinyurl.com/zdvjxd7 (Walsh, Morgan, & Mahlan, 2011)
- Increasing Our Presence in the Emerging Markets
  http://tinyurl.com/h44ofv6 (Menezes, 2013)
- OECD Indicators, Innovation and Technology
  https://data.oecd.org/searchresults/?r=%2Bf%2Ftype%2Findicators&r=%2Bf%2Ftopics_en%2Finnovation+and+technology (OECD, 2015)

Potential Uses of the Case

The case can be used to explore and teach product positioning and the environmental analysis focusing on social, competitive dynamics. Especially focusing issues in emerging market environments, market and customer segmentation, the fit between different marketing strategies and alternative market/product positions can be explored with different scenarios in during and after the completion of the M&A.

Answer with Analysis of all Assignment and Discussion Questions

1. **The spirits market was growing in Turkey but slower than other emerging markets. Did Diageo made the best decision to simply enter the Turkish market with acquisition, or should it try to expand its existing operations organically in Turkey pushing its international brands?**
   With its large population (~70 M), high urbanization and growing economy Turkey had been an appealing market for investors for many years. It had also been in the radar of Diageo for a number of years, as the disposable income levels increased, middle-class rapidly grew and approximately 1 M people reached the legal drinking age each year. Turkish spirits market had grew at an average rate of 4% from 2006 to 2010 (Exhibits 4 and 5). Compound annual growth rate (CAGR) of Turkish Rakı market had increased from 1.1% in year

2005 to 7.8% in year 2010 (Exhibit 11). Similarly, CAGR of Turkish Vodka market had enjoyed even a higher growth from 7.5% in year 2005 to 15.1% in year 2010 (Exhibit 13). Before the Mey Içki acquisition, Diageo had a healthy share of the whisky category, which had a compound annual growth rate (CAGR) of 5.4% between 2006 and 2010. Scotch whisky was the first foreign product to be registered and protected as a 'geographical indication of origin' in Turkey in 2011, and Diageo's J&B and Johnnie Walker brands accounted for over 60% of the category. However, whisky accounted for only the 5.9% of the overall market in Turkey (Exhibit 6).

Rakı was a totally new to Diageo. Undertaking an alcohol operation in an emerging but predominantly Muslim country ruled by a religiously inclined government is also an experience for Diageo.

First the M&A faced tax issues, due to increased taxation approach on alcoholic beverages.

Diageo and other foreign liquor companies have been in a six-year customs dispute in Turkey, which caused Diageo to halt shipments to the country for the past six months. Liquor importers have been asked to pay more customs tax on spirits imported into Turkey between 2001 and 2009. Diageo's custom-tax bill could exceed £100 million, or about US$160 million, according to the company's annual report (Cimilluca, 2011).

Then further troubles followed, *"two years after the deal, Turkey's government enforced a law forbidding advertisements and restricting sales of alcohol"* (Finkel & Buckley, 2015).

Lastly, the predominant brand position came with other costs mostly related to monopolistic acquisitions. *"In June 2014, the competition board fined the company 41.5 million liras ($14.9 million) for breaching competition rules"* (Finkel & Buckley, 2015).

On the other hand, the M&A had given Diageo a change to transforms its position in this attractive emerging market, which had high growth, and high margin business. Mey icki, with an enterprise value of TL3.3 billion (£1.3 billion) has provided an attractive acquisition with an accretive earnings per share for the first year, and 13% weighted average cost of capital for the 5 year outlook (Diageo, 2011).

2. **A market analysis of Turkey would include a qualitative and quantitative evaluation. Based on the information in the case and other information that you can collect on the Internet, which quantitative figures would be most important for the market analysis? How would market potential and market concepts apply to your analysis?**

Diageo faces unstable economy, government restrictions, and counterfeit products in Turkey as a developing country. Volatile economic conditions cause an extra risk level and uncertain returns on investment for Diageo. Government restrictions such as ban on alcohol advertising hinder the ability for Diageo to gain market share and brand recognition in this new market.

Diageo has significant brand strength in the premium spirits segment, with an extensive product portfolio across categories and price points, and widespread production facilities. However, the stringent advertising regulations (Sonne & Cimilluca, 2011), the booming trade of counterfeit alcohol (Cihan, 2015; Harvey, 2011; O'Toole, 2005; Taylor, 2015), and its dependence on third parties for its raw materials impose certain limitations.

3. **As part of the environmental analysis, what environmental forces are in favour and against Diageo's acquisition or the spirits market in general in Turkey?**

   All external variables, including political, social, economic, technological, and semi-controllable other forces that have an impact on the industry should be carefully monitored for the environmental analysis. As presented in Fig. 1, PEST Analysis could be completed for an environmental analysis.

4. **Develop a preliminary competitive/industry analysis for spirits market in Turkey. What are major advantages and weaknesses of Diageo/Mey, when compared with the competition?**

   First levels of competition needs to be identified, from the closest and most intensive competitors to those most distant, namely any competitor that customers may switch to should be included. In this regard, Exhibits 5, 6, 11 and 14 provide detailed comparison of competitors.

5. **What complications emerge from analysing the spirits market in Turkey, as compared with analysing the spirits market in your country or in the US?**

   Students are expected to refer to political, economic, social and technological differences inherit in their home country market.

6. **What brand/product positioning does Yeni Rakı hold for which targets?**

   Brand/product positioning refers to the place, the brand/product holds in the minds and hearts of consumers. The target audience, the good/service offered, the frame of reference/category, and the points of differentiation/uniqueness are often its components.

   Rakı, in total, holds 25% of the total alcohol market by value (Exhibit 5), seconding beer at 57%. Rakı generated ~23 M USD export income in year 2010, again seconding beer. However, beer category is also an import item while rakı preserves its legacy as an export only item in the foreign trade (Exhibit 6). Rakı provides the highest total sales in Diageo spirits portfolio by 77%, while Yeni Rakı has a 64% market share among all rakı brands of Diageo (Exhibit 11). Yeni means "new", as it is the second rakı brand by TEKEL, which started in 1944, when the Turkish state monopolized the rakı production. It has 45% alcohol and made of dry and fresh grapes, fresh aniseed and water. It has historical and popular value and it is also the rakı brand with highest levels of export Exhibit 14). It's sold at 43.50 TL, priced at 0.9% of the rakı segment average. Yeni Rakı is known as THE RAKı with its unique selling point, and targets all consumer groups (Exhibit 9).

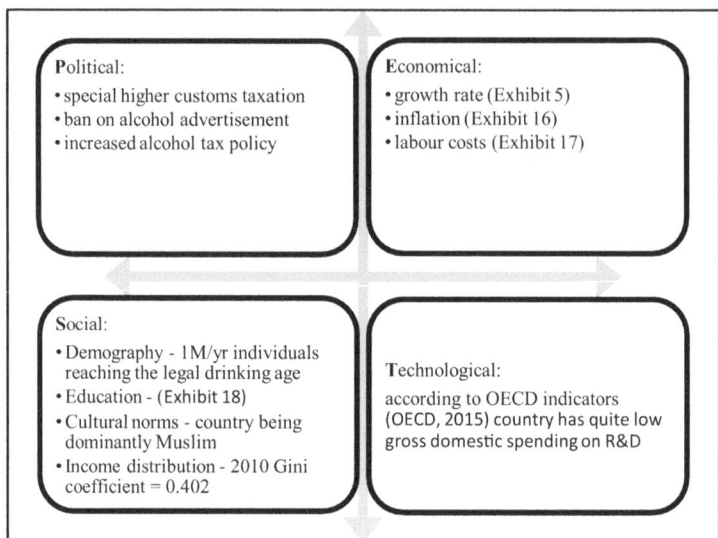

Fig. 1 PEST analysis

Suggested Teaching Approach

We recommend assigning some of the questions and dividing the classroom into groups for group discussion. Groups should be assigned to same set of questions and should discuss their position first internally. Based on the discussion, each group than makes a brief presentation of their answer(s). After each group completes their presentation, entire classroom discusses the issues in the case/questions.

In order to help students make reading and research at home, this case and questions of choice can be given as home assignments, after or before the creation of case discussion groups. If assigned as homework, the case groups can be established among students with similar answers to save time on group dynamics and presentation preparation.

Audiovisual Support Material (Where Applicable)

- Diageo Focused on Emerging-Market Expansion
  http://www.bloomberg.com/news/videos/b/dad4b239-bb47-4132-8420-67ebc3d466ba (Walsh, 2011)
- Morgan Says Mey Icki Gives Diageo a Platform in Turkey
  https://www.youtube.com/watch?v=obAAV5NrPbk (Morgan, 2012)
- Turkey competition board opens probe against alcoholic beverage company
  https://www.youtube.com/watch?v=hC7h6C2Eigk (Mindreader, 2015)

Proposed Session Plan

- Introduction Diageo and its global strategy including Mey Merger (30 min)
- Break (5 min)
- Introduction to Turkish alcohol market, its categories and players (20 min)
- (Re)introduce discussion questions of choice (10 min)
- Break (5 min)
- Discussion (20 min)
- Formulation of the discussion summary (20 min)

References

Cihan. (2015). *Two people die due to bootleg alcohol in western Turkey*. Retrieved from http://en.cihan.com.tr/en/two-people-die-due-to-bootleg-alcohol-in-western-turkey-1960348.htm
Cimilluca, D. (2011). *Diageo to Buy Turkey's Mey Içki*. Retrieved from http://www.wsj.com/articles/SB10001424052748704271104576156612353607144
Diageo. (2011). *Acquisition of Mey İçki*. Retrieved from http://www.diageo.com/Lists/Resources/Attachments/738/Diageo%20Announcement%20-%20FINAL.pdf
Finkel, I., & Buckley, T. (2015). *Diageo's Turkish unit under investigation by competition board*. Retrieved from http://www.bloomberg.com/news/articles/2015-08-11/diageo-s-turkish-unit-under-investigation-by-competition-board
Fletcher, C. (2011). *Diageo to Buy Turkish Distiller Mey Icki for $2.1 Billion*. Retrieved from http://www.bloomberg.com/news/articles/2011-02-20/diageo-said-to-be-close-to-buying-distillery-mey-icki-of-turkey
Harvey, B. (2011). *Counterfeit alcohol kills Russian guide in Turkey*, Vatan Says. Retrieved from http://www.bloomberg.com/news/articles/2011-05-31/counterfeit-alcohol-kills-russian-guide-in-turkey-vatan-says
Harvey, B., & Fletcher, C. (2013). *Diageo seeks Turkey drink limit balance after Mey Icki purchase*. Retrieved from http://www.bloomberg.com/news/articles/2013-05-16/diageo-seeks-turkey-drink-limit-balance-after-mey-icki-purchase
Menezes, I. (2013). *Increasing our presence in the emerging markets*. Retrieved from https://www.diageo.com/Lists/Resources/Attachments/1601/Review of our acquisitions in the emerging markets_transcripts.pdf
Mindreader. (2015). *Turkey competition board opens probe against alcoholic beverage company*. Retrieved from https://www.youtube.com/watch?v=hC7h6C2Eigk
Morgan, A. (2012). *Morgan Says Mey Icki Gives Diageo a Platform in Turkey*. Bloomberg Business.
O'Toole, P. (2005). *Fake alcohol causes Turkey deaths*. Retrieved from http://news.bbc.co.uk/2/hi/europe/4336005.stm
OECD. (2015). *Indicators, innovation and technology*. Retrieved from https://data.oecd.org/searchresults/?r=%2Bf%2Ftype%2Findicators&r=%2Bf%2Ftopics_en%2Finnovation+and+technology
Schweizer, K., & Hacaoglu, S. (2013). *Turkey's liquor market at risk*. Retrieved from http://www.bloomberg.com/bw/articles/2013-06-20/turkeys-liquor-market-at-risk
Sonne, P., & Cimilluca, D. (2011). *Diageo Takes Gamble on Turkey With Mey Buy*. Retrieved from http://www.wsj.com/articles/SB10001424052748704476604576158183882692162
Stock, K. (2013). *Diageo's $2.1 Billion Turkish Hangover*. Retrieved from http://www.bloomberg.com/bw/articles/2013-06-24/diageos-2-dot-1-billion-turkish-hangover

Taylor, P. (2015). *Counterfeit alcohol kills 19 in Istanbul*. Retrieved from http://www.securingindustry.com/food-and-beverage/counterfeit-alcohol-kills-19-in-istanbul/s104/a2574/%20-%20.VmmO8bh97Dc

Walsh, P. (2011). *Diageo Focused on Emerging-Market Expansion*. Bloomberg Business.

Walsh, P., Morgan, A., & Mahlan, D. (2011). *Diageo to acquire Mey Icki Q&A: Diageo*.

Teaching Note: Case 5: To Switch or Not to Switch—Madhu's Dilemma

Shashi Shekhar Mishra and Arijit Pathak

Synopsis

On 2 September 2012, Madhu has once again received a SMS, on her registered mobile number from the local cable operator, reminding her to install Set Top Box (STB), in order to continue hassle free viewing of her favourite television programs. Installing STB would improve the quality of picture, but Madhu's monthly budget would also increase—as she will have to pay based on the number of channels or bouquet of channels subscribed. Recently, she also came across an advertisement of Airtel Digital TV, a national-level DTH service provider. She has collected the information about various options on the internet and through her acquaintances over last few days. Now she is focused upon making a choice between local cable operator versus Airtel and deciding the suitable package considering the family needs. Madhu's dilemma is to contain the monthly subscription bill without compromising on the quality of her family's TV viewing experience. Now, she is wondering whether her decision can be solely based upon economic value of offerings and all other benefits can be ignored in the choice of DTH services.

Teaching Objectives

The three primary teaching objectives are:

1. To demonstrate the triggers and barriers to consumer switching behaviour and discuss the importance of various factors in determining a consumer's choices of a DTH service.

S.S. Mishra (✉) · A. Pathak
Department of Industrial and Management Engineering, Indian Institute of Technology Kanpur, Kanpur, Uttar Pradesh, India
e-mail: ssmishra@iitk.ac.in; aripat_iitk@yahoo.com

2. To discuss how consumers evaluate DTH services. The role of quantitative analysis is highlighted to assess the value of all competitive offerings.
  3. To demonstrate the linkages between consumers behaviour insights and formulation of marketing strategies for services.

Use of the Case

This case has been written to exhibit various aspect of consumer decision making process in Indian context. The case suits well to be included in consumer behaviour module of basic Marketing Management course, offered in the first-year of MBA. It can also be used in Services Marketing courses to help participants understand various concepts of consumer behaviour relevant specifically to services *vis-à-vis* physical products.

Assignment Questions

1. What are the triggers and barriers to a customer's brand switching intent for Cable TV/DTH services?
2. Compare various options that Madhu have based on their monetary value?
3. Will she opt for Cable and Satellite mode of transmission offered by local cable operator? If yes, then why and if not, then why not?
4. How the brand image of national DTH service providers would influence Madhu's decision?
5. As a marketing strategy for local cable operator, what can further be done to prevent Madhu from switching?
6. How can other DTH companies attract the existing customers of a rival company?

Teaching the Case: Brief Overview of Analysis and Discussion

Analysis of the case is divided into four parts:

- Triggers and barriers to a customer's brand switching intent Cable TV/for DTH services
- Evaluating the monetary cost of various options to Madhu
- Reasons why Madhu should switch or not, considering monetary and non-monetary benefits
- Implications for marketing strategy to retain the customers and attract switchers

1. Triggers and barriers to a customer's brand switching intent for Cable TV/DTH services

The protagonist of case, Madhu, has to make a decision about whether to continue with existing local cable service operator or switch to new DTH service providers. The complexity of decision making is multiplied by the fact that Madhu is looking to optimize the bundled service and quality of service vis-a-vis price. The case can be opened by posing a question to the class that what prompts customer to leave a service provider. Based on own past experiences and word-of-mouth, participants can answer the question and instructor can list various triggers of switching a service provider including higher subscription price of Airtel Digital TV and lower price of competitive offering. According to Keaveney (1995), the antecedents to customers' service switching behaviour include eight factors, *viz.*, Price, Inconvenience, Core Service Failure, Service Encounter Failures, Response to Service Failure, Relatively Attractive Competitive offering, Ethical Problems, and Involuntary Switching. On the other side, there are a number of barriers to a customer's brand switching intent including additional monetary cost of new set top box, accessory materials and installation charges, time and effort required for change over, and uncertainty about the other alternatives.

At this point of time, instructor should provoke a discussion on how consumer evaluation processes differ between Goods and Services. Extent of ease or difficulty in evaluation of products before purchase is considered to be function of its attributes, based on which there are three types of products, *viz.*, High on Search attributes, High on Experience attributes, and High on Credence attributes Zeithaml (1981). Most of services fall in the category of either experience or credence type, which means that customers find it difficult to evaluate them before purchase and hence degree of perceived risk is high in purchase decision making process. Uncertainty about the quality of alternative service providers makes customer susceptible about switching to other options and they tend to stay with existing service provider. Customers' 'passive' attitude of staying with existing service provider can be attributed to perceived switching barriers than because of a higher level of satisfaction, indicating a lengthier zone of tolerance. At this point, instructor can collate the list of triggers and barriers to consumers' switching behaviour by showing Table 1.

In the case, Madhu has been prompted to think about DTH connection, by an SMS from the local cable operator, informing her to install Set Top Box which would directly result in a hike in monthly subscription fee. The price hike has come at time when she is contemplating the idea of having buying second TV set with additional connection option. This may increase her monthly spending on TV viewing than what she believes is appropriate and hence she wants to evaluate all options. She had a couple of options, *viz.*, switching to DTH service providers, installing a STB connection from local cable operator, opt for a more economical packages or build her own A-la carte package *vis-à-vis* staying with current subscription plan. Madhu's decision will depend upon her evaluation of all the options based on their relative value measured through monetary and non-monetary benefits and cost considerations.

Table 1 Triggers and barriers to consumers' switching behaviour

Triggers[a]	Barriers[b]
Price • Higher Package Price • Frequent Price Increases • Unfair Pricing • Deceptive Pricing	Performance Risk • Transmission quality • Continuity in service • After sales service
Inconvenience • Disturbance in transmission • Low reliability of hardware • Wait for service	Evaluation Cost • Time cost • Effort Cost
Core Service Failure • Abrupt channel off • Billing Errors • Service Catastrophe	Set up cost • Cost of new hardware (set top box etc.) • Cost of un-installing old hardware • Installation charges
Service Encounter Failures • Uncaring • Impolite • Unresponsive • Incompetent	Brand relationship loss cost • Personal Relationship Loss Costs • Affective losses associated with breaking the bonds of identification
Response to Service Failure • Negative Response • No Response • Reluctant Response	
Competition • Suitable package design • Better prices	Personal Barriers • Lack of knowledge about other options • Deprivation stage of mind
Ethical Problem • Charging extra without prior information • Higher prices than informed • Hidden charges • Hard Sell	
Involuntary Switching • Services unavailable to customer's new location • Provider closed	

[a]Adapted from Keaveney (1995); [b]Adapted from Burnham et al. (2003)

2. Evaluating the monetary cost of various options to Madhu

First, it is important to assess the need of Madhu's family and determine the channel requirements of the family as whole. From the case facts, her family's channel requirements include:

- Hindi Entertainment (Colors, Life OK, Zee TV, Sony, Star Plus)
- Kids Channels (Cartoon Network, Pogo, Disney, Disney Kids, and Nickelodeon)
- Infotainment (Discovery, Animal Planet, National Geographic Channel or History TV 18)

- News (Times Now, CNBC TV18, Bloomberg and ET Now)
- Sports (ESPN, Star Sports, Star Cricket, Ten Sports, Ten Cricket and Sony Six)
- Devotional (Aastha and Sanskar)
- Lifestyle and Music Channels (MTV, Bindass, and Zoom)
- Hollywood Movies (Star Movies, HBO and WB)

The options available to Madhu are as below:

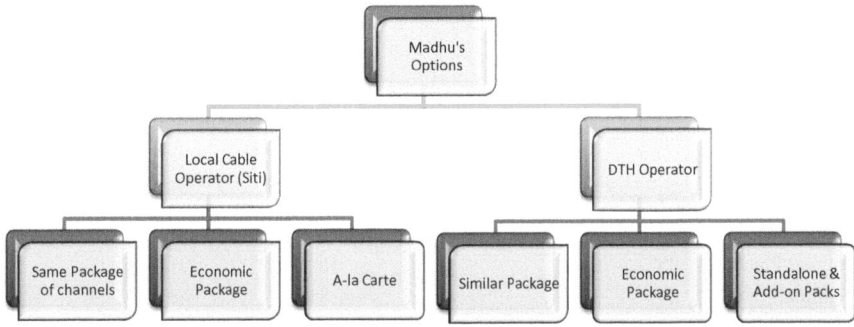

Madhu's choices may have variations at two levels- Channel Package and service provider. She can choose either a more economical channel package or make her own a-la carte based on her family's need; else she can retain the same package under local cable operator or switch to similar type of package with other DTH service provider. To evaluate various options, first we enumerated the cost of all the channels, desired by her family member, across all DTH/Cable TV service providers. The details about the calculation are given in Table 2 (using Case Exhibit 2 and 6) and it is quite evident that even if Madhu just subscribes to her family members bare minimum requirements through A-la Carte/standalone mode, still she will end up paying more than what is she is paying now. Therefore, simply subscribing to individual channels will not provide her any monetary benefits.

In second option, she can choose one of the different packages offered by the Cable Operator through CITY CABLE (MSO) or Airtel Digital TV. If she exercises this option, she has to make sure that either the subscribed package should have all the channels desired by her family members or she had to additionally subscribe to those individual channels that are not the part of regular channel package. With this condition, we have calculated the total cost of channel package by simply adding the cost of a regular monthly package with the cost of channels that are not included in a regular monthly package across all service providers (use case exhibit 1, 2, 4, 5 and 6). An additional excel sheet provided with this teaching note provides the detailed calculation about the same and Table 3 summarizes the result of the analysis.

From the above given analysis, it is quite evident that all the regular packages of different service providers cannot meet Madhu's current requirements in terms of monetary cost, except Airtel Mega and CITY CABLE's Popular, Grand and Premium packages. However, it is worth considering that just based on the

Table 2 A-la Carte/Standalone Subscription Cost across various service providers

Channels	Channel subscription fee in Airtel/Month (INR)	Channel subscription fee in CITY CABLE/Month (INR)
Colors	25	13
Life OK	20	12
Sony	25	8
Star Plus	20	12
Zee TV	20	12
Cartoon Network	25	12
Pogo	25	12
Disney	25	9
Discovery Kids	20	11
Nickelodeon	25	7
Discovery	25	12
Animal Planet	25	15
National Geographic	20	8
History TV18	25	16
Times Now	15	8
CNBC TV18	15	7
Bloomberg	10	7
ET Now	10	7
ESPN	45	24
Star Sports	45	22
Ten Sports	40	15
Ten Cricket	40	20
Aastha	10	3
Sanskar	5	3
MTV	15	7
Bindass	10	11
Zoom	15	6
Star Movies	25	16
HBO	30	17
WB	30	10
Total Cost	685	342

difference in monthly cost, she can't switch to any of these plans. There are various qualitative factors that have to be taken in consideration along with package cost to decide the best option. The instructor can build a matrix like Table 4 for evaluation of different options on various criteria that turn up during the course of the class discussion.

Table 3 Cost of various packages to fulfil family channel requirements

Service provider	Package title	Monthly subscription fee (INR)	Cost of additional channel not included in package (INR)	Total monthly subscription cost (INR)
Airtel	Value Sports	220	355	575
	Economy Sports	300	100	400
	Mega	350	0	350
	Ultra	430	0	430
CITY CABLE[a]	Janta	100	378	537
	Popular	170	181	394
	Grand	222	53	309
	Premium	267	7	308

[a]Indicates that the Total Monthly Subscription Cost for the service provider does not include tax (@12.36%) in channel prices and has been added separately

Table 4 Overall evaluation of different options available to a customer

Criteria/Options	Option-1	Option-2	Option-3
Monthly Charges			
Installation Charges			
Service Charge			
Package Design			
Quality of After Sales Services			
Transmission Quality			
Payment Terms			

3. Reasons why Madhu should switch or not, considering monetary and non-monetary benefits

Besides monetary cost, there are various non-monetary factors that affect a customer's choice of a service. Also, seldom a customer may indulge in an extensive cost analysis as we have performed to evaluate each of the options as above and therefore, customer knowledge and involvement plays a critical role in the comparison of various options. In this case, Madhu may know CITY CABLE options and Airtel Mega as comparatively more economical, but she will also consider the other factors such as initial price of a set top box and installation cost, perceived quality of service provided by CITY CABLE or Airtel, brand value of Airtel/CITY CABLE and convenience in use of Airtel/CITY CABLE applications. Hence, Madhu's final decision will be influenced by relative value of each competitive offering.

At this point of time, instructor can pose a question about what constitute perceived value for a customer.

Perceived Value = f (Perceived Benefits ~ Perceived Cost)

While Airtel Mega may have higher cost over similar competitive options from CITY CABLE but Airtel may definitely be rated better over its transmission quality, support services, and brand value. Local Cable TV operators have one of their biggest drawback in their quality of transmission and support service (Recall the incidence of little Gauri visiting Madhu's home to watch TV as her cable operator has removed the channel without any prior notice). There is also a consideration of switching cost attached with changing service provider and therefore an estimation of the same has been done below:

Minimum Monthly Subscription in Different Platform

Sl. No	Name of Platform	Name of Package	Min. Monthly Subscription	Additional Charges (for installation)
1	Airtel Digital TV[a]	Mega (Rs. 350 per month)	INR 350	INR 2200 (INR 2000 + INR 200)
2	CITY CABLE	Premium (Rs. 267 per month)	INR 308	INR 1600 (INR 900 + INR 700)

[a]Airtel Digital TV on installation offers one month free subscription of 150 channels worth INR 300

If switched to Airtel Digital TV:

Additional Installation Cost: INR 2200
Free Subscription for 1 Month: INR 300
Additional Cost to be incurred/month = INR (350 − 275) = INR 75

If adopts CITY CABLE option:

Additional Installation Cost: INR 1600
Additional Cost to be incurred/month = INR (308 − 275) = INR 33

At this point, an instructor can leave the judgement to individual participant on whether Madhu will switch or not. Instructor can also pose a question on why class does not have an agreement in opinion.

4. **Implications for marketing strategy to retain the customers and attract switchers**

Based on the above analysis, implications for marketers can be divided in two categories, *viz.*, how to retain your existing customer and how to catch switchers. Before the class indulges in any discussion, an instructor can point out following reasons for retaining the existing customer:

- Acquiring a new customer could be five times costlier than retaining an existing customer
- Customer's value tends to increases as relationship prolongs
- Cost of serving customers decreases with operational efficiency and learning

Implication for retaining your loyal customers is to create more value for them. Customers will not necessarily switch for low cost options, rather they will appreciate better support service and custom designed solutions (channel packages in case of DTH services). The best way to build switching barriers for your customers is to provide them flexibility and support in making choices. On the other side, the best way to attract switchers is lower their switching cost by providing warranty of services, waiving-off re-installation charges and cost of new set top boxes on subscription for a minimum time period. During discussion, participants can also come up with their innovative ideas to attract potential switchers.

Post Script

Madhu has recently switched to 'Mega Pack', having a monthly subscription fee of INR 350, under Airtel Digital TV.

While deciding, she thought it would be better to switch to Airtel Digital TV, as it provides better flexibility in choosing packages, offers better services and convenience of online payment. The incidence related to Gauri also played a very important role in materialization of her decision.

References (Suggested Readings)

Keaveney, S. M. (1995). Customer switching behavior in service industries: An exploratory study. *Journal of Marketing, 59*, 71–82.

Zeithaml, V. A. (1981). How consumer evaluation processes differ between goods and services. In J. H. Donnelly & W. R. George (Eds.), *Marketing of services*. Chicago: American Marketing Association.

Burnham, T. A., Frels, J. K., & Mahajan, V. (2003). Consumer switching costs: A typology, antecedents, and consequences. *Journal of Marketing, 31*(2), 109–126.

Teaching Note: Case 6: Funmax 4D Animation Theatre

Rashmi Malik, Kalpit Shah, Brahmeswarar Yerrabolu, Harikumar B. Varrier, Sumit Bhat, and Atanu Adhikari

Synopsis

FunMax4D is located in the Garuda Mall in Bangalore which is at the heart of Bangalore city's M.G. Road area. Garuda mall in Bengaluru is a crowd puller and its proximity to several known areas in Bengaluru. But with advantages of the location, and high number of people vising the mall, FunMax4D hasn't been able to have profitability. The rental rate at Garuda mall is extremely high and is one of the factors impacting the profitability of FunMax4D.

Total space rented at Garuda Mall is 2000 sq. ft. out which some portion is not used. FunMax4D tried to use this for video games or other entertainment but did not succeed. It would really help if the total area is 4000 sq. ft. or so to venture into

---

R. Malik (✉)
Hewlett Packard Enterprise, Madhapur, India
e-mail: rashmi.malik@yahoo.com

K. Shah
Paladion Networks, Mumbai, India
e-mail: kalpitshah85@gmail.com

B. Yerrabolu
Director of Engineering - Capture Product Development, Altisource, Bangalore, India
e-mail: brahmeswara@yahoo.com

H.B. Varrier
Home Business, Philips Lighting, Chennai, India
e-mail: HARIKUMAR.B@gmail.com

S. Bhat
Paladion Networks, Mumbai, India
e-mail: s.bhat81@yahoo.com

A. Adhikari
Department of Marketing, Indian Institute of Management Kozhikode, Kozhikode, India
e-mail: Atanu.Adhikari@iimk.ac.in

© Springer International Publishing AG 2017
A. Adhikari, S.K. Roy (eds.), *Instructor's Manual for Strategic Marketing Cases in Emerging Markets*, DOI 10.1007/978-3-319-52697-3_6

related entertainment services provider for funzone activities like mirror maze, scary house (these are other activities that FUnMax4D is capable of providing as in their other operations, these are provided).

FunMax4D pays about Rs. 120 per sq. Foot as a rental cost currently at Garuda Mall. There is not much space to expand to add additional activities like mirror maze and scare house. These would have contributed to the additional revenues with less operational expenses.

FunMax4D tried to establish additional unit in Bengaluru at Soul Space mall (new one opened on Marthahalli, Outer Ring Road, Bangalore in 2011) but due to difference of opinion amongst the partners the expansion idea was dropped. This would have given FunMax4D some flexibility to bargain with Garuda Mall owners or close the Garuda Theater and move to Soul Space.

Misled by auditors and due to lack of experience FunMax4D got categorized under cinematography instead of amusement category. Entertainment tax under cinematography is 30% on revenue compared to amusement category which is around 17%. This is one of the major issues impacting the overall profitability of FunMax4D.

Mr. Murthy is in dilemma as what to do next. FunMax4D profits are not as expected. The challenges;

- Improve Profits
- Entertainment tax
- Lack of larger area to expand additional revenue generating activities like gamezone, mirror maze etc.
- High Rental Cost
- Urgent issues to be addressed are either to sell or continue

Case Objectives

The case is structured to achieve the following objectives.

1. To assess the viability of a substantial investment by FunMax4D in setting up the 4D theater.
2. To bring out the challenges in differentiation and repositioning strategies in a highly competitive environment.
3. To identify and evaluate several strategic alternatives for FunMax4D to come out of the current position and exploit a strong market opportunity that is likely to solidify in the near future.
4. Calculate the economic value to customers to justify the premium that the company charges. The challenge, however, is to communicate this value to customers who may not be well educated but very experienced and set in their ways.

Analysis: In Class Discussion

SWOT

The SWOT analysis of FunMax4D is as below:

Strength	Weakness
• Location Advantage • Access to huge number of customers • First mover advantage • Well informed and technically sound stakeholders	• No clear strategic direction • Non frequent content change • Falling profits • Dis harmony amongst stake holders • Not much inculcation of the concept amongst the customers • Government policies
Opportunities	Threats
• Serve Additional customer group • Expand content offering to meet broad range of customers interest • Diversify into related services • Faster market growth • Add complimentary offerings	• Likely entry of new competitors • Emerging substitute offering by other vendors entering into this business • Probability of rental rates increase • Changing stakeholders choices

Segment (Figs. 1 and 2)

From the segment wise analysis we can conclude that FunMax4D should target the following (Fig. 3):

- FunMax4D should broaden its segment base and also focus on Tier 2 cities.
- Malls have just arrived in these cities. People have the tendency to visit the new establishments. FunMax4D can maximize current profits.
- The purchasing power in these cities has been on the rise.

Current Segmentation	Future Segmentation
Geography: Tier 1 Cities Hyderabad, Bangalore	Geography: Tier 1 &Tier 2 Cities Tier1 : Hyderabad, Bangalore Tier 2 : Coimbatore, Mysore, Baroda, Pune
Place: Mall	Place: Mall, Planetariums, Edutainment Centres
Age: 5 - 9 yrs and 18 – 35	Age: 5 - 9 yrs and 18 - 35
Education: School Children, Literate crowd.	Education: School children, Literate crowd.
Family size: Young, Young married, Young married with child under 10	Family size: Young, Young married, Young married with child under 10

Fig. 1 Comparison of current and future segmentation

Segment – wise analysis:

	Measurable	Substantial	Accessible	Differential	Actionable
Tier 1 Cities	High	High	Medium	High	Low
Tier 2 Cities	High	Medium	High	Medium	High
Mall	High	Medium	High	High	High
Planetarium	Medium	Low	High	Medium	High
Theme Parks	Medium	Low	High	Low	Medium
Expos	Low	Medium	High	Low	Low
Edutainment Centers	High	Medium	High	High	High
Age: 5 - 9 yrs	High	High	High	High	High
Age: 18 -35	High	High	High	High	High
School children	High	High	High	High	High
Literate Crowd	High	High	High	High	High
Family size: Young, Young married, Young married with child under 10	High	High	High	High	High

Fig. 2 Segmentation criteria

Geography: Tier 1 &Tier 2 Cities Tier1 : Hyderabad, Bangalore Tier 2 : Coimbatore, Mysore, Baroda, Pune
Place: Mall, Planetariums, Edutainment Centres
Age: 5 - 9 yrs and 18 – 35
Education: School children, Literate crowd.
Family size: Young, Young married, Young married with child under 10

Fig. 3 Segmentation criteria

Target Strategy

FunMax4D should adopt a **Product Specialization** targeting pattern.

As show in Fig. 4, **FunMax4D has a single product—4D film(s) which it can use it to target different markets—malls, planetariums, edutainment centers.**

Positioning
- **Flexible market offering for FunMax4D**: FunMax4D should go with a flexible market offering which provides a **naked solution**—offering customers to view 4D movies along with **discretionary option** of playing video games outside the theater premises of a mall.

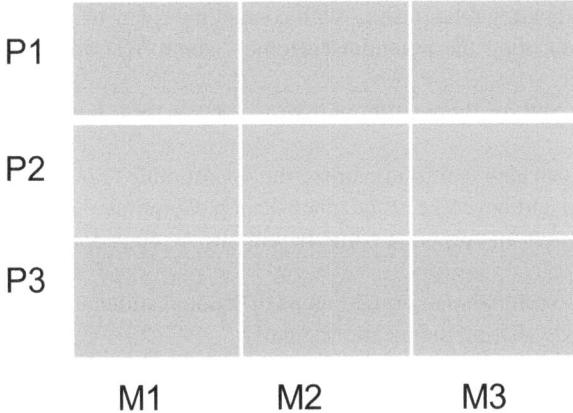

Fig. 4 Product Specialization strategy of FunMax4D

- Also, they should screen movies without the 4D effect when the theater capacity is low. This is as good as watching a 3D movie and can save a lot of cost.
- In order to reduce the cost of the 4D games, it will help to partner with upcoming 4D owners in other cities.

Product
- FunMax4Dshould diversify the range of 4D films including Educational movies and should be available to the students throughout the year.
- Theatre should also be playing 3D films in addition the 4D films to allow for feature films in excess of 150 min.
- More market penetration should be achieved by extending the current base only in commercial multiplexes to commercial destinations, Educational institutions, various shows and workshops and getting established in Tier 2 cities.
- FunMax4D Employees should be trained in a better way to connect with customers and focus on "customer intimacy." More focus should be given towards greeting the customers with a smile, enthusiastically welcome customers to the theatre, establish eye contact and try to remember customers' names if they are frequent customers.
- FunMax4Dshould ensure that their theatre is place for a family entertainment spot with children's play and themed celebration area giving importance to family gatherings birthdays and so on.
- Thus Funmax4Dshould create a new brand identity by offering unique and superior services, an interactive experience, aiming at Convenience and simplicity with a stunning best-of-class audience experience.

Price
- Increasing the ticket price may not be wise to gain profits since the current price charged falls under affordable limits of the crowd that is expected to visit Garuda Mall.

- Maintaining healthy relationships with content providers to reduce the operating costs and educating the potential customers about 4D can successfully bring more profits.
- The Unique Selling Proposition will be to have a wide number and quality of films.
- FunMax4D can also aim to maximize the opportunities to increase the revenue through food and beverage at the cinema shop. Corporate level discounts to get more business from corporate partners will also be considered.

Promotion

- Towards Promotional marketing, Funmax4Dshould stimulate Customers to take action towards visiting the theatre regularly.
- Towards achieving this, various incentives to attract Customers should be designed in the form of Contests and create awareness in the new Customers.
- Funmax4Dshould focus on the hybrid promotional strategy i.e. a mix of pull and push strategy.
- They should have more advertisements in local newspapers and billboards and should give higher discounts to stimulate immediate sales.
- Budgets should be reserved for other sales promotions that include coupons, samples, premiums, point-of-purchase (POP) displays, contests, rebates, and sweepstakes for schools, tourists, and corporate groups.
- An additional Sales Promotion should be planned by offering complimentary discounted food coupons along with the tickets, since there is a Food zone on the same floor.
- There isn't a formal public relation office yet, but should be established to manage public relation while interacting with corporate customers.
- Direct marketing may not be a feasible option as it requires additional skills and cost.
- Some events such as appearance of celebrities related to the film should be planned in the theatre to attract mass media attention.
- Funmax4Dshould focus to work on underserved communities and look for solutions for their upliftment activities.
- They should execute corporate social responsibility programs through partnerships with nonprofit organizations (NPOs) and non-governmental organizations (NGOs).
- Also options like Individual Gifting solution could be evaluated. The gifting solution can be in the form of coupons or pre-paid vouchers which can be purchased and used.
- Volume discounts for educational institutes could be looked as an option.

Place

- Funmax4D must create a desire to the customers to re-visit the theatre to enjoy the changing programs. To achieve that they should create a stall in the main lobby of Garuda Mall to make aware of the theatre and the movie(s) details. The stall personnel should also be able to educate the ones who are not having much idea about the 4D technology and the movie.

- There should be options created for online purchasing of the tickets to avoid the rush and making it convenient for the customers who travel far distances. FunMax4D should have its own website or partner with mediatory websites like bookmyshow.com. Website should also be frequently updated with the show timings and listings. It should continue to provide information on the experience, current and forthcoming titles and daily session times.
- They should tie up with other entertainment shops to include more gaming, sporting events and any other live events.
- In the long run Funmax4D will build its heritage of immersive, high-quality educational and entertainment movies presented in prestigious institutions and destination centers by increasingly expanding its network into more commercial destinations.

Profitability Analysis: Worst Case, Medium Case and Best Case Analysis

From Exhibit 5 (foot fall in Garuda mall) in the Funmax4D Case document, we evaluate the below to be the Worst case, Medium case and best case profits as below.

4D Theater BIS	Seat arrangements			Rate Per seat (INR)	Revenue projections		
	Best	Medium	Worst		Worst (INR)	Medium (INR)	Best (INR)
Weeknd (per month)—conv 2%	8000	6400	3200	80	256,000	512,000	640,000
weekday (per month)—Conv 1.5%	8800	6600	4400	70	308,000	462,000	616,000
					564,000	974,000	1,256,000

Teaching Note: Case 7: Managing Social Media Communications at Garanti Bank

Kaan Varnali, Evrim Ersoy, Sezin Gul Tanriverdi, and Elif Terzi

Case Synopsis

The case study starts with a conversation involving the Executive Vice President of Garanti Bank and the head of Social Platforms Management Unit providing the plot for the rest of the case study. The background section follows the introduction section, where background information regarding Garanti Bank in general and the social media landscape in Turkey in banking industry in particular is provided. Overall brand positioning strategy of Garanti Bank, along with the existing social media communication strategy that aims to support the overall brand positioning strategy is explained in detail. Detailed information regarding the key performance indicators (KPIs), how Garanti Bank monitors these KPIs and the competition in the local banking industry in social media are provided. Examples of content shared by Garanti Bank in social media and the interaction rates belonging to these contents are provided. Finally, the case concludes with providing a detailed conversion rates for each of the products that the bank is trying to generate leads on social media for the years 2014–2015. What is expected from the students is to both develop suggestions on how the brand may increase its interaction rate in line with its strategic targets and decide on the optimum portfolio of banking products that is most suitable for lead generation on social media. In doing so, students are expected to analyse and evaluate the effectiveness of Garanti Bank's approach in social media management in conveying brands' core values and generating leads on social media.

K. Varnali (✉)
Faculty of Communication, Istanbul Bilgi University, Istanbul, Turkey
e-mail: kaan.varnali@bilgi.edu.tr

E. Ersoy • S.G. Tanriverdi • E. Terzi
Social Platforms Management, Garanti Bank, Istanbul, Turkey

Learning Outcomes

- Understand the goals and key performance indicators of social media marketing.
- Identify and critically evaluate insights on which ideas for marketing communication activities in social media can be built upon.
- Build an operational plan for customer engagement on social media.
- Understand the prerequisites and the difficulty of establishing both a sustainable and profitable presence in social media.
- Appreciate the value of digital platforms in customer relationship management.
- Understand the primary drivers of interaction in social media.

Suggested Readings

- Ashley, C. and Tuten, T. (2015). Creative Strategies in Social Media Marketing: An Exploratory Study of Branded Social Content and Consumer Engagement. *Psychology & Marketing*, 32(1), 15–27.
- Brodie, R. J., Ilic, A., Juric, B., & Hollebeek, L. (2013). Consumer Engagement in a Virtual Brand Community: An Exploratory Analysis. *Journal of Business Research*, 66(1), 105–114.
- Deighton, J. & Kornfeld, L. (2009). Interactivity's Unanticipated Consequences for Marketers and Marketing. *Journal of Interactive Marketing*, 23, 4–10.
- Grinnel, C. (2009). From Consumer to Prosumer to Produser: Who Keeps Shifting My Paradigm? (We Do!). *Public Culture*, 21(3), 577–598.
- Hollebeek, L.D., Glynn, M.S. & Brodie, R.J. (2014). Consumer Brand Engagement in Social Media: Conceptualization, Scale Development and Validation. *Journal of Interactive Marketing*, 28, 149–165.
- Kozinets, R (2014). Social Brand Engagement. *GfKMir*, 6(2), 8–15.
- Peters, K., Chen, Y., Kaplan, A.M., Ognibeni, B. & Pauwels, K. (2013). Social Media Metrics—A Framework and Guidelines for Managing Social Media. *Journal of Interactive Marketing*, 27, 281–298.
- Schamari, J. & Schaefers, T. (2015). Leaving the Home Turf: How Brands Can Use Webcare on Consumer-generated Platforms to Increase Positive Consumer Engagement. *Journal of Interactive Marketing*, 30, 20–33.

Potential Uses of the Case

This is a library case that requires secondary research. Although the case includes extensive information necessary for the decisions to be made, students will gain much from conducting a thorough research on social media activities of Garanti Bank, its local competitors, plus other global banks. This case provides the background for creative thinking on social media marketing. It involves issues such as content marketing, customer care in social media, converting traffic in social media channels into product leads, brand engagement in social media, and assessment of interaction rates. Not only these issues constitute the hot topics in the industry, they are also very new in the academic platforms as well. Therefore, this case could be potentially used in graduate level marketing courses in MBA, Executive MBA, communication, media, and advertising programs. Further, the case may also be used in corporate training programs.

Proposed Session Plan

- Start the session with a discussion on how to be a social brand based on the framework offered by Kozinets (2014).[1]
- Moderate a discussion on how Garanti Bank performs when compared to the standards of a social brand (Kozinets, 2014) (see footnote 1).
- Refering to Hollebeek, Glynn, & Brodie (2014)[2] establish an understanding that brand engagement in an individual level requires appealing to both cognitive and emotional aspects, which reflects on behavioural tendencies.
- Zooming in on the case, ask students to evaluate marketing activities of local competitors (as shown in Table 1) on social media to have an overall understanding of the Turkish banking industry.
- Moderate a discussion on how Garanti Bank performs in social media when compared to local competitors.
- Refering to Ashley & Tuten (2015)[3] assess how Garanti Bank performs in terms of managing branded social content.
  Ask students to compile a list of banking products and assess their weaknesses and strengths in terms of their fit with social media. Prioritize the products to which leads will be generated in your action plan.
- Finally, ask students to present their action plan on how to increase the interaction rates of branded content, while increasing leads generated on social media.
- End the session with a brief assessment of learning outcomes.

Suggested Discussion Questions

Discussion Question 1

Is social media being utilized to its full potential?

---

[1] Kozinets, R (2014). Social Brand Engagement. GfKMir, 6(2), 8–15.

[2] Hollebeek, L.D., Glynn, M.S. & Brodie, R.J. (2014). Consumer Brand Engagement in Social Media: Conceptualization, Scale Development and Validation. Journal of Interactive Marketing, 28, 149–165.

[3] Ashley, C. and Tuten, T. (2015). Creative Strategies in Social Media Marketing: An Exploratory Study of Branded Social Content and Consumer Engagement. Psychology & Marketing, 32(1), 15–27.

Answer for Discussion Question 1

Before the session, students should be encouraged to benchmark global banks in terms of social media management strategy.

In the context of social media relationships, engagement practices are either led by customers or brands. Further these relationships vary in terms of their degree of intimacy and excitement. Building upon these premises Kozinets (2014)[4] provides a comprehensive framework in which he summarizes four general strategies for successful and positive social brand engagement. First one is customer care, which often involve use of social media to monitor customer requests and complaints and to provide customer service through social media. Customer care strategy embraces a customer-led engagement practice and helps building intimacy into the relationship. Well-crafted customer care programs provide a basis for comfort and intimacy in a brand's social media presence. As referred in the "Garanti Bank in Social Media" section of the case, @GarantiyeSor is such a customer care initiative and helps channeling complaining customers to appropriate customer-service personnel. Further, effective social media monitoring helps prevent "forest fires", in other words, PR scandals and social media crises.

The second strategy is communication and sharing, which involves an array of a company-led engagement practices such as sharing news about the company, products and promotions, commercials and advertising. In these types of practices the goal is facilitating word of mouth marketing by publishing stimulating and exciting content in various forms, which when spread by consumers, influence other consumers to purchase and use more of the brand's products and services. As referred in the Interaction Rates section of the case, Garanti's content marketing and advertising practices fall into the domain of this strategy.

The third strategy is co-creation, which requires a sophisticated approach in content marketing. In co-creation strategy, the brand should learn to gather ideas from consumers and collaborate in the creative endeavours. Co-creation requires innovation in communication practices, because it leads to consumer-created brands. The communication messages are crafted by consumers within a campaign designed specifically to facilitate consumer involvement upon a key insight gained from consumers' experiences and world. Therefore, a successful co-creation approach often requires both listening and real-time responding capabilities on social media on behalf of the brand. Further, it requires the brands to understand that effective social media management requires a shift from "control" to "influence" (Peters et al., 2013)[5]. Garanti seldom engages in co-creation activities.

Finally, fourth strategy is communing and listening, which involves the use of social media to listen widely and deeply to consumer conversations related to

---

[4]Kozinets, R (2014). Social Brand Engagement. GfKMir, 6(2), 8–15.
[5]Peters, K., Chen, Y., Kaplan, A.M., Ognibeni, B. & Pauwels, K. (2013). Social Media Metrics — A Framework and Guidelines for Managing Social Media. Journal of Interactive Marketing, 27, 281–298.

brands. Communing and listening provides the ability to establish mutually understanding and intimate relationships in social media. From the tables and exhibits provided in the case it is seen that Garanti Bank engages in some level of communing and listening.

Discussion Question 2

Try to identify the unique nature of customer voice in social media in banking industry. What can be done by the Bank to effectively manage the overall sentiment around the Garanti brand in social media?

Answer for Discussion Question 2

Customers submit complaints to the firm to accomplish a change in the practices, policies, or offerings of the firm and/or to seek some form of remedy. Prior to social media, complaining has never been the dominant customer reaction to dissatisfaction. Several reasons pertaining to this fact are the time and effort required to submit a complaint to the firm, not knowing where or how to complain, nearly perfect competition, or believing that the manufacturer or retailer will not do anything about the problem.

With the advent and proliferation of social media, anecdotal evidence suggests that, being a political action, complaining fitted smoothly with the nature of consumer activism on social media. Consumers increasingly use social media to interact with the firms they buy from, as well as other consumers, to take an active role in co-creating market offerings. In doing so, dissatisfied customers complain, sometimes bitterly, about a variety of customer-service issues on social media creating a negative chatter. Further, the relative ease of posting a complaint on social media exacerbates both the number of complainers and the complaints. This chatter includes (1) the complaints that would have been submitted directly to the firm or to third parties in the absence of social media, (2) complaints that wouldn't find its way to the firm or a third party due to aforementioned inhibitors of action, and (3) the negative word of mouth in the form of consumer protest generated by outraged consumers.

Banking sector is a typical example of a service industry, in which switching costs, especially in terms of customer effort and time, are high, and the costs associated with the service provided (e.g., credit card membership fees, account maintenance fees, fees associated with leases and loans) are perceived as unjust; therefore customers tend to complain. Although customers publicly complaining on the Internet have been mainly conceived as protesters who are engaging in negative word of mouth to persuade the public to oppose a firm, it is not always the case. Today, the line separating the conceptual boundaries of submitting a complaint directly to a company and complaining to masses becomes thinner, as customers increasingly adopt social media as the primary channel for voicing their complaints and expect firms to have effective listening and responding capabilities online. Therefore, many of those complaint instances (in other words negative chatter) are actually customer requests framed in the form of a complaint. @GarantiyeSor is a social media practice that aims to manage this phenomenon. It is a customer care platform, as well as a listening and communing channel. Operators of @GarantiyeSor opens a dialogue between the company and the dissatisfied customer to provide the necessary intimacy in the one-to-one relationship to resolve the conflict situation, before it starts a viral negative chain reaction among similar dissatisfied customers on social media.

Further, enjoyable and life-style focused content publishing also serves as a trigger for positive engagement. Such content often attracts positive comments and are shared among users with relevant interests, creating an organic reach and positive brand associations.

Discussion Question 3

Identify market segments and prioritize marketing efforts targeting these segments in line with the goal of increasing interaction rates. Try to assess which segments will be more inclined to emotionally engage with which kinds of content shared in social media.

Answer for Discussion Question 3

Banks, as many other mass service provider firms, often serve to a wide range of customer profiles including customers with diverse demographics, lifestyles, cultural backgrounds, risk profiles, etc. Therefore, establishing a communication strategy that fits them all in official social media accounts presents a huge problem. A viable way to tackle this problem is to establish an official tone for all outbound communications from the official accounts, yet at the same time to generate different content publishing strategies for particular groups with differentiating needs. For instance, targeting youth, Garanti has a viral content strategy called "Experimental Banking" (in Turkish Deneysel Bankacilik). It has a separate Facebook page (https://www.facebook.com/DeneyselBankacilik/). Humorous videos are published in Youtube and Vimeo, together with illustrations and graphics in Facebook. In each of the videos Garanti brand is mentioned. Additionally, Garanti has a separate tab in its official Facebook page for women entrepreneurs, publishes practical tips and how-tos for rookie investors, and pleasant lifestyle content for average Facebook users. However, as underlined in almost all reference articles, interaction rate actually is a function of content relevance and entertainment. Hence, students shall benefit much from identifying market segments and aligning social media content strategy with the specific needs of these constituencies.

Discussion Question 4

What should be Garanti Bank's approach in its pursuit of increasing the number of leads to its products?

Answer for Discussion Question 4

Success in generating leads in social media is driven by three factor: (1) the success of the creative content strategy, (2) effectiveness of user experience design, (3) employing a product portfolio that is suitable for lead generation in social media.

First, an effective creative content strategy allows links for product application forms embedded in branded content to meet with potential customers in social media. Content refers to the information delivered by social media, which can be either functional (i.e., tips on how to succeed in short term investment) or hedonic (i.e., entertainment). Creative aspects of branded social content should be designed in a way that maximizes psychological engagement with the customer. A branded social content strategy that accomplishes this objective should bridge the gap between what the marketer wants to say and what the consumer needs to hear (Ashley & Tuten, 2015).[6] It encompasses both message content (e.g., use of humor, sexuality, unexpectedness, emotional appeals, richness and relevance of information) and execution (e.g., timing, channel selection, frequency of communication). The overall creative content strategy must be designed in a way that increases the likelihood it can produce the desired effects in the target audience.

Second, the navigational experience of the customer should be designed in a way that increases the likelihood the customer completes the desired action flow to generate a successful product lead. This phenomenon falls into the domain of user experience design. The journey which starts at the instance when a user notices a branded content in social media, continues with him somehow reading, watching, or playing with the content, coming across the embedded link to the product application within the content or in the platform that hosts the content, clicking the link to reach the application form, to ultimately fill and submit the form must be designed meticulously to provide a seamless, easy to use, preferably short, non-intrusive, and somewhat entertaining experience. Students should be encouraged to evaluate each of the customer journeys they could find in the social sphere designed by the Garanti Bank, to come up with suggestions to improve the conversion rate across the journey.

Finally, students shall be encouraged to compile a list of banking products and assess their weaknesses and strengths in terms of their fit with social media. As

---

[6]Ashley, C. and Tuten, T. (2015). *Creative Strategies in Social Media Marketing: An Exploratory Study of Branded Social Content and Consumer Engagement. Psychology & Marketing, 32(1),* 15–27.

explained above, an effective creative content strategy is a key determinant of customer attention and engagement in social media. Therefore, products that can either be a part of the storyline of an engaging social media campaign or at least fit well within the plot of a branded content can be considered as having potential for generating leads in social media.

Teaching Note: Case 8: Revolution Ventures—Introduction to the Service Organization and Situation Description

Gautam Roy and Atanu Adhikari

Case Synopsis

The company **Revolution Ventures** was founded in September 2009 with an initial capital of Rs. 10,000. It is a proprietary firm registered in Ahmedabad. The proprietor—Krishna Rungta has had rich exposure in the field of IT. It was his desire to contribute to the education sector given the lack of quality and affordable technical education available to the masses in the back office of this world. The trigger for Krishna was his struggle in finding easy and free source of educational material when he wanted to take up GRE or when he wanted to have an in-depth understanding of languages like SAP or Java during his professional career.

Krishna launched his first website Guru99.com which provided an excellent stepping stone for people in Quality Assurance. On the success of this, he created two off-shoots of the site dedicated for JAVA and SAP.

His recent venture is the MegaVocab site which is providing a path breaking way for students to learn English.

There are three different products that Revolution Ventures has to offer. These are:

1. Open Source Education—http://www.guru99.com/, http://www.javatutorialhub.com/

   The websites present learning materials for various open source software like Java, LoadRunner, QualityCenter and QTP. It covers more practical aspect of the usage which is very useful for professionals who have just started in this field

or professionals who have considerable experience but are stuck in a situation and need quick resolution leveraging knowledge of other professionals in the forum. There are various interview questions and tests to challenge the technical skills.
2. Unique vocabulary learning technique—http://www.MegaVocab.com/
   The website presents a revolutionary vocabulary learning technique which uses the strengths of different learning strategies to ease vocabulary learning. It contains videos that explain the words in a thematic format and the person after going through the conversation identifies the meaning of the word.
3. SAP Training—http://www.saptraininghub.com/
   SAP is one of the products which command a very high premium in the market. A practice version of the software will be available for interested candidates to try their hands on the product. It is a very unique concept as the product license is very expensive and it is not possible for everyone to purchase the product.

Revolution Ventures intends to grow into a global company and is therefore looking to create a marketing strategy that would enable to increase the eyeballs to the Website as well as engage the visitor who has visited the site thereby increasing the number of loyal customers.

Teaching Objectives

1. Strategic Leadership—Managing the strategy making process for Competitive Advantage
2. Identification of Opportunities and Threats
3. Competitive Advantage through business level strategy
4. Possible Strategies for core Technical industries

Level of Program Where the Case Is to Be Taught

1. Managers with some background in Strategy.
2. Awareness of basic principles a must for an in-depth understanding and analysis of the case.
3. Executives at cross-roads to determine priorities.

Suggested Assignment Questions

Revolution Ventures intends to grow into a global company and is therefore looking to create a marketing strategy that would enable to increase the eyeballs to the Website as well as engage the visitor who has visited the site thereby increasing the number of loyal customers.

We are required to develop an effective marketing strategy for Revolution Ventures for short term, medium term, and long term.

Recommended Readings

1. The Strategy Concept and Process: A Pragmatic Approach—Hax, Arnoldo C., and Nicolas S. Majluf
2. Christensen, C. The Innovator's Dilemma: When Technologies Cause Great Firms to Fail
3. Strategic Management—An integrated approach—Hill & Jones

Suggested Discussion Questions

1. How do you determine an organization's core competence and position a product based on its core competence?
2. What is Logical incrementalism?
3. At what stage, do you assign priorities to Market Penetration or Product Development? How are these priorities defined?

The case may be given as a pre-read, the instructor should start with the suggested discussion questions and then move ahead with the detailed analysis—expected time to analyse the case in detail is 1.5–2 h. Groups in 3–4 people should be asked to present the case and provide solutions.

Consumer Behaviour

Michael Solomon in his book on Consumer Behaviour has referred Consumer Behaviour as study of the process involved when individuals or groups select, purchase, use, or dispose of products, services, ideas, or experiences to satisfy needs and desires.

Understanding consumer behaviour is of outmost important to Revolution Ventures as it would help it to do better business for sure. Firms exist to satisfy needs and Revolution Ventures is no exception to it. It can only satisfy these needs to the extent that it understands the people or organisations who will use the product of services of Revolution Ventures, hence it is quite pivotal for Revolution Ventures to establish the needs of the market segments that it caters to and channelize its efforts accordingly to make sure that the value offered to its customers are always the best in the industry and incremental.

Revolution Ventures needs to establish the wants of the different segments that it targets for its Products and Services like Open Source Education and SAP Training, and MegaVocab. The target audience of Revolution Ventures comprise of serious users who seek material to enhance their career or profession and would generally engage with the Websites that enable them to achieve these objectives.

The different Consumer Groups of Category 1 audience for Revolution Ventures Products and services are:

- Students who have acquired their basic educational qualifications and are looking for certifications in the areas of applied areas to enable them to build their career.
- Students of vernacular medium who need to learn English to enable them to enhance their career path.
- Teachers of schools and colleges who could use the Website as supplementary site to enable them as well as their students to gain mastery on the subject.
- Professionals looking to make a shift in their domains due to attractiveness and demand of the new domain.
- Practitioners of the domain looking for supportive site to seek guidance and knowledge to enable them to solve the issues encountered in the profession.
- Students aspiring to appear for GMAT/GRE.
- Students with vernacular background who want to learn the language to grow in their career.
- Practitioners in the Industry who would like to expand their vocabulary.
- Teachers of schools and colleges who need to use this site as a support to their lectures.

The typical behaviour of these audiences can be categorized in the following manner:

- Low attention span
- Browsing through the sites listed within the top 20 in Google Search or any other Search Engines
- Looking for serious and authentic contents
- Engaging with sites that provide them the latest and up-to-date contents
- Prefer to exchange their views through discussion forums to validate the learning as well as to seek solutions to their issues in hand
- Would prefer free contents that are good and authentic, supporting their career objectives

The different consumers of Category 2 audiences are:

- Publishers and Sellers of Books on the relevant topics
- Certification agencies offering professional certifications
- Companies selling supplementary tools that could help the audience in achieving their career objectives and aspirations
- Other Websites who are not competitors but sell supplementary services/ products
- Institutes offering certification examinations

- BPOs and SAP Consultants looking for professionals with relevant skills

  Generic behaviour of the above consumers could be represented as follows:

- Would like to associate with Websites that supplement their products
- Would like to associate with Websites that has large number of visitors who could be potential buyers of their products
- Seek value for money for the investments made
- Would look for quick results and are impatient in terms of results
- Would like to pay based on results-pay for sales made, not for impressions

Marketing activities exert an enormous impact on individuals and Revolution Ventures needs to get this act right as well, providing the right level of stimulus to its advantage. Thus the marketing strategy of Revolution Ventures needs to be based in consideration of the above behaviours of its consumers. We have formulated the strategy in the sections to follow based on this study.

Understanding the Case

While the services to Category 1 audience is being offered free of charge, it forms the basis of success of Revolution Ventures because based on the number of subscribers, engaged users, and popularity of Website the Category 2 audience would make their business decision whether to advertise their Products and Services on the Revolution Ventures Website, thereby resulting in the requisite revenues for Revolution Ventures to sustain and grow the business and hence the emphasis on Category 1 audience since without that audience the Category 2 audience will not sign up.

Let us understand the Category 1 audience related target segment for two products

1. Open Source Education and SAP Training

The target segment for this product comprises of the students who have passed out of colleges after acquiring basic qualifications to start a career and are therefore looking for the career oriented applied technology sites that can provide them the requisite knowledge and certifications that are recognized in the Industry to make them employable.

A different set of target audience for this Product comprises of the practitioners and employed professionals who would like to get into the domain of SAP due to its high recognition, potential, and emoluments.

A Third category of audience for this Product are the practitioners of SAP who are looking for solutions to the technical issues faced on course of their jobs to be able to resolve the issues faced or to learn new concepts.

This Product needs to cater to the three types of audiences described above and therefore would have different flavours to offer to meet the requirements of these audiences. For example, while affiliation with Certifying Agencies recognized for SAP Certifications would be necessary to target the student category as well as professionals looking to move into this domain since they would require the necessary professional certification that is recognized by the Industry for their career advancement, for SAP practitioners, a discussion forum and blogs from experts would be offered to engage them gainfully. The bottom line to engage this target segment is to have valuable, in-depth contents, that is useful in the profession and the requirements of all three categories of target audience will be addressed.

2. MegaVocab

Target audience for this Product comprise of

- Students aspiring to appear for GMAT/GRE
- Students with vernacular background who want to learn the language to grow in their career
- Practitioners in the Industry who would like to expand their vocabulary
- Teachers of schools and colleges who need to use this site as a support to their lectures

This Product will be structured to cater to the requirements of all four categories of audience and will engage them effectively. Teachers can form a strategic part of this Product because if they like this Product and find the Website useful, they would recommend this Website to their students, which will increase the visitors as well as enable this audience to engage themselves. These students in turn can spread the word of mouth to their families, relatives, friends, and acquaintances creating a chain reaction which will enable to draw the critical mass to the site.

MegaVocab would thus be structured to allow all four types of target segment to be tapped and engaged by having "Expert Advice" section wherein Teachers and Language Experts would be invited to express their advice on the subject and method to improve vocabulary and made the learning attractive. Discussion Forums would enable the audience to engage in worthwhile communication and exchange of learning needs, learning experience, career opportunities, etc. and Blogs would enable expression of latest developments, learning methods, and techniques. Above all, the Website will allow only authentic and relevant contents and therefore every entry will be strictly moderated and if necessary, edited to ensure compliance to the objective of being a serious and professional site only for serious audiences.

In terms of Category 2 audience, the market segmentation needs to be done for the following types of users:

- Publishers and Sellers of Books on the relevant topics
- Certification agencies offering professional certifications

- Companies selling supplementary tools that could help the audience in achieving their career objectives and aspirations
- Other Websites who are not competitors but sell supplementary services/products
- Institutes offering certification examinations
- BPOs and SAP Consultants looking for professionals with relevant skills

Revolution Ventures should aggressively mark their efforts towards Substantial Innovation and Incremental Innovation in its product offerings. Their products Open Source education, SAP training and MegaVocab can be put through the substantial innovation and incremental innovation cycles so as to make their product offerings in the eLearning space always pertinent and one which increasingly adds upon its value offerings to its customers at all times. Offering these value offering free of cost reinforce its uniqueness.

The company should focus on its customer needs which would help it constantly yield important information for it to determine key value opportunities for new product development. Customer satisfaction indicates how well the product use experience compares to the value expected by the user, the closer the match between expectations and the use experience, the better is the resulting value. Revolution Ventures needs to make a difference in trying to exceed the customer expectations at all times.

If we take an example of the SAP training they should always be the first to make available the latest SAP training material pertaining to the latest release in the SAP world so that it can attract more potential users. By its industry leading offerings, bringing in more value to its customer base and keeping it abreast with the latest technological advances it will be able to deliver the unique product which will help in retaining the customer.

Targeting and Positioning

Effective targeting and positioning strategies are essential in gaining and sustaining superior organizational performance. The market targeting decision identifies the people or organization in a product market toward which an organization directs its positioning strategy. Selecting good market targets is one of the management's most demanding challenges. Targeting and positioning strategy consists of

- Identifying and analysing the segments in a product-market
- Deciding which segment(s) to target
- Designing and implementing a positioning strategy for each target

The two products being considered by Revolution Ventures is provided free of cost and the company intends to attract consumers by capturing as many eye balls as possible. Let us analyse these as per the steps defined above to derive the strategy.

Identifying and Analysing the Segments in a Product-Market

In terms of Category 1 audience, target segment for Open Source Education and SAP Training has been specified in the previous section of this paper. This segment thus comprise of serious users who would be interested in factual and serious contents that will enable them to learn the topics and build their core competence in this area.

Based on the knowledge acquired, they would like to get into this practice and choose this practice as their career path. Again, the target segment for MegaVocab has been specified in the previous section of this paper. This audience is also of serious type who would like to be with a dependable site which can help them to structure their career path.

Students and young aspirants have low attention span and search Google for relevant materials. They need serious and good material to be attracted to the Website and to hold their attention and build loyalty. Secondly, this audience have low pocket money and would definitely be attracted to free and quality contents if available.

In terms of Category 2 audience, target segment would be Certifying Agencies, Book Publishers and Sellers, Websites providing supplementary information, Companies selling supplementary tools, BPOs and SAP Consulting Companies.

Deciding Which Segment(s) to Target

Management needs to decide whether it will target a single segment, selectively target a few segments, or target all or most of the segments in the product-market. Several factors influence the choice of the targeting strategy:

- Stage of product-market maturity
- Extent of diversity in buyer preferences
- Organizational capabilities and resources
- Opportunities for gaining competitive advantage

e-Learning is at the growth phase wherein various companies are coming up with innovative ideas for setting up e-Learning Websites. However, these Websites start-up with initially attractive contents but after a period they fail to attract visitors due to stagnant contents which are not updated regularly or they start lacking in quality of contents being provided to the visitors. Moreover, most of these sites are paid or subscribed sites charging a fair sum of money.

In this product-market, the buyer preferences are towards genuine and serious contents since they are willing to be attached to sites that provide them the necessary quality contents that are regularly updated for them to be dependable because the buyer is putting their future career at stake.

Since the audience for the products are students, young aspirants, professionals, teachers, and practitioners, they should be targeted across the regions.

For the Category 2 audience, they should be targeted across the regions as well and the Website should be positioned as no nonsense site where the contents are carefully moderated and edited before publishing including the contents of discussion forums, blogs, etc. so that the audience of Category 1 are engaged with this site and the site gains popularity through reference and word of mouth publicity. Similarly, the teachers should be prompted to use this site as reference and advise their students to use this site as a learning supplement.

Designing and Implementing a Positioning Strategy for Each Target

As per Cravens and Piercy, the industry environment is influenced by the extent of concentration of its firms, the stage of its maturity, and its exposure to international competition. They have indicated that following five general environments portray the range of industry structures:

- Emerging
- Fragmented
- Transitional
- Declining
- Global

These five categories are neither exhaustive nor mutually exclusive. The e-Learning Industry is in the emerging state due to the application of new technology, the changing needs of buyers, and the identification of unmet needs by suppliers.

The buyers' preferences in this market are similar which limits segmentation efforts. The industry structure is such that new enterprises are more likely to enter the market than the large, well-established companies. More successful firms have been charging the customers for the kind of resources that Revolution Ventures is offering whereas Revolution Ventures has emerged with quality products that is offered free to the customers. The objective is to have maximum number of subscribers so that the other companies view this as an opportunity to market their products and services to the subscribers of Revolution Ventures by advertising on their site for which Revolution Ventures will charge revenues.

Integrated Marketing and Communications

- SEO activities which would enable to place the Website very high on the search engine search results. Under this strategy, all the relevant and important key words are covered and the site is popularized through organic methods. The

main focus is Google search engine however other search engines are also targeted.
- The Website encourages people to share their experience in social networking sites and there are pages created in twitter, facebook where people can share their experiences about the website. The people can also use their facebook/twitter credentials to say that they "like" the contents and they can also book mark the contents
- The Viral marketing concept is being used to promote the videos especially for the MegaVocab site. One word capsule is sent in email and it contains the details of the website. People who like the capsule share it with their family and friends and this in turn generates traffic to the site as people are intrigued to see more such videos.

Recommended Marketing Strategy

Marketing strategy consists of analysis, strategy development and implementation activities in:

- Developing a vision about the market(s) of interest to the organisation
- Selecting market target strategies and setting objectives
- Developing, implementing and managing the marketing program positioning strategies designed to meet the value requirements of the customers in each market target.

Recommendations:
1. The site is based on the concept of free contents. There are many people who have a mentality that free contents are crap. Therefore we recommend that the main focus of the product should be on contents. The contents should be such that people who land on the site are able to gauge the richness of contents and are engaged to the site.
2. The content richness is aimed to create a direct competition with the paid sites where the user start realising that they are able to get similar/if not better contents from this site and will stop subscription to the paid sites
3. Revolution Ventures should follow a market driven strategy where the development of the contents should be taking into account a constantly changing business environment that it operates in and on the need to deliver superior customer value at all times. Their focus of strategic marketing should be organisational performance and its marketing strategy should seek to deliver superior customer value by combining customer-influencing strategies of the business into a coordinated set of market-driven actions.

4. Revolution Ventures is serving a variety of users like students, professionals, etc. They have to consistently provide expertise in business environment monitoring the customer groups and provide the right experience. For example for the SAP training product of Revolution Venture, it should constantly analyse and monitor the requirements which are most valuable to its primary customers so that they derive value out of the Revolution Ventures' offerings and this would then catapult it to be a market leader in SAP training in this product segment.
5. The revenue model is based on advertising and so it is very important that the advertisers get the right value. The contents of the advertisements should be well placed i.e. the selection of the keywords should be right. For e.g., just a vanilla certification will result in advertisements showing certifications for drawing, painting, etc. whereas the users would be expecting searches on SAP certifications.
6. Though the model is advertisement based revenue model, there needs to be a perfect balance between the contents and the advertisement. Too much of advertisement such that the essence of content is lost and users get distracted from the site will lead to dissatisfaction of the user. For e.g. in the video if the advertisement is more than 30% of the entire video then the user will think of it as a drag and they may switch over to other content rich sites instead of watching the next video. This will also happen if the same advertisement is repeated.

Short Term Strategy

- Just the good and unique contents of Revolution Ventures will not help unless there is a continuous effort to get more contents into the site. Also, the quality of the contents need to be worked upon and maintained in order to engage the users and attract their loyalty.
- The presentation of the site needs to be simple and should be a "no nonsense", "no frills" type and the user should be able to find any contents with at most two clicks from anywhere within the site.
- The SEO activities need to be carefully planned based on the analysis of most searched keywords on the topics and also think of complex keyword searches so that in all cases the site should be ranked amongst the top 20 sites with appropriate landing page. This will help in drawing more users towards the site.
- Revolution Ventures is also engaged in a kind of social marketing by having fan pages in Facebook and LinkedIn. However they need to extend this further to sites like Twitter, which is preferred by the top executives and professionals and would enable the users to share their experiences through these sites. This is likely to create a viral effect where more users will be able to know about the website and will be drawn towards the product.

- Revolution Ventures should tie-up with other websites to create two-way traffic. There are various link sharing options available and prudence should be applied in selecting appropriate forums such that it does not dilute the seriousness and image of the site.

Medium Term Strategy

The biggest hurdle is to constantly update the Website. Therefore resources should be dedicated to perform this task and the progress needs to be reviewed by the Senior Executives to ensure seriousness. The contents should be thoroughly scrutinised and validated before publishing. The quality of the contents cannot be compromised at any stage. The recommended method to get the contents is:

- Users create contents: Create a group and discussion forum within the site so that the user can extend their knowledge by sharing with others. This will not only engage the users but will also encourage knowledge sharing thereby creating contents for the site automatically. However, the contents shared should be scrutinized to maintain the desired Quality Standards before publishing.
- Experts create contents: Revolution Ventures should establish a tie-up with the Subject Matter Experts (SME) to engage with the site. This will need locating the SME and inviting them to the site. The simplicity and authenticity of site with knowledge sharing capabilities should be attractive enough to entice these experts and engage them once they visit the site. Users will be able to post their queries to these SMEs, who will help the users to resolve their queries faster. By sharing their expertise on the Website SMEs would have a good opportunity to display their knowledge and experience and would therefore be approached by the Corporate for various assignments. This will create a win-win situation.
- Create daily capsules that can be emailed to the members. This will enable people to get the latest updates on the contents as well as serve as a teaser to visit the site for details on the topics. Besides, the mailers will also create a new revenue generation opportunity as a couple of advertisements could also be placed within the mailer.

Long Term Strategy

Apart from SAP training, Revolution Ventures can create a space containing shared licenses where the users can actually practise the SAP commands. Since the license is expensive, it will not be possible for everyone to purchase the license. However pooling the resources will help as it will result in a cheaper option for the users and Revolution Ventures will be able to get a new source of revenue generation.

As per the discussion with the proprietor it seems that they are interested in expanding their operations in US. We feel that this should be a later priority and can be considered as long term objective than a current priority.

Apart from expanding in geographies it will be good to get venture funding so that the marketing budget can increase and they can advertise in an elaborate manner. This will help in acquiring new customers faster and in expanding the business.

We would like to re-iterate that though this is a free website, Revolution Ventures should focus on the quality and authenticity of contents such that it should be of a quality comparable if not better than any paid services Websites. The seriousness to maintain such quality contents need to be maintained throughout.

Teaching Note: Case 9: M-PESA: A Renowned Disruptive Innovation from Kenya

Isaac K. Ngugi and Lilian W. Komo

Case Synopsis

This case study describes the developments and success of M-Pesa. M-Pesa is the first banking app for mobile phones to be developed in the developing world. It was designed by Safaricom limited Company in Kenya The product has received global attention due to its uniqueness, innovativeness, rapid adoption, and the impact it has made to a large population, mostly people who are poor (bottom of pyramid). M-Pesa has many uses, including: transfer of money from person to person, buying airtime, paying utility bills and keeping the money in the M-Pesa account for future use. The product connected a population which was hitherto disconnected from accessing financial services. As an early mover in mobile banking in Kenya, Safaricom limited company partnered with other businesses thereby broadening its agent network before competitors came into the scene. M-Pesa is a disruptive innovation, having created a new market and value network and disrupting the existing ones and becoming a major competitor against the established market leaders and alliances in the financial services sector in Kenya.
List of Teaching Objectives

- Upon reading the case study, students should be able to:
    - Define the term disruptive innovation
    - Describe the characteristics of disruptive innovation
    - Describe the key factors attributable to successful design, development and marketing of a new product

Level of program where the case to be taught (MBA, Executive Education programme)

I.K. Ngugi (✉) • L.W. Komo
Faculty of Management, The Business School, Bournemouth University, Poole, UK
e-mail: ingugi@bournemouth.ac.uk

- Either undergraduate or postgraduate university level

Suggested Assignment and Discussion Questions:
 (i) Define the term disruptive innovation.
  - Suggested points could include in the answer:
    – A disruptive innovation refers to the "process by which a product or service takes root initially in simple applications at the bottom of a market and then relentlessly moves up market, eventually displacing established competitors. A disruptive innovation is an innovation that creates a new market and value network and eventually disrupts an existing market and value network, displacing established market leaders and alliances (Wikipedia)."

 (ii) What are the characteristics of a disruptive innovation?
  - Suggested points could include:
    – According to Jiwa (2015), the following are the characteristics of disruptive innovations.
    – Start with a purpose and a small problem rather than a big idea.
    – Based on what people do, not what they say they do.
    – Leverage data to get closer to users, customers or fans.
    – Can be more responsive to customer's behaviours and needs.
    – Tap into consumer's latent desire.
    – Connect the disconnected.
    – Create value where none existed.
    – Disrupt people not industries—changing the user's worldview and behaviour.
    – Begin by changing a small group of people at the edges.
    – Seem obvious only after the fact.

 (iii) Describe the key factors attributable to successful design, development and marketing of a new technological product.
  - Suggested points could include in the answer:
    – Thorough market research to identify consumer need
    – Develop simple to use products
    – Target a sizeable segment
    – Value co-creation through partnerships
    – Invest in promotion of the product
    – Develop or use effective distribution channels

Suggested Readings
- Omwansa T. and Sullivan N. (2012) Money, Real Quick: The story of M-PESA. Guardian shorts.

- Trott P. (2011) Innovation Management and New Product Development. 5th ed. London: Financial Times Prentice Hall.

Potential Uses of the Case

- Discussion is seminar sessions in class or in a participatory lecture.

Answer with analysis of all assignment and discussion question (see part 'd' above for answers to the questions provided).

Suggested teaching approach—Could provide the case study to students in advance so that they read in private time. Then meet and discuss the case study as well as the questions and answers.

Audiovisual support material (where applicable)

- M-PESA documentary https://youtu.be/zQo4VoLyHe0
- How M-Pesa Business caught President Barack Obama's attention https://youtu.be/6UQGg1LWJFU
- The M-Pesa Revolution https://youtu.be/G5eOT9-olgU

Postscript

The growth of M-Pesa has continued within Kenya and now even internationally. People can now send money from other countries such as US and UK to Kenya via M-Pesa. Safaricom limited company has also continued to grow. In 2014, it was rated the most profitable company in Kenya. M-Pesa was the force behind this great achievement, powering the company to attain the top position countrywide (Kenyan Daily Nation newspaper, May 13th 2014—http://mobile.nation.co.ke/news/Safaricom-profit-hits-Sh23bn/-/1950946/2312386/-/format/xhtml/-/15pik9gz/-/index.html).

Teaching Note: Case 10: Irrway—A Green Personal Mobility Solution

M.S. Chandrashekar, Gaurav Sharma, Basant P. Rangadhol, Ashwin Petkar, Mohan Mookan, and Atanu Adhikari

Synopsis

Anjan and his firm Greendzine Technologies Pvt. Ltd. (GTPL) have created enough stir in some of the market segments like Golf Courses and Mall Complexes with the Irrway™ product. They need to be able to decide whether to take a shot with the upcoming opportunity to serve the mall segment for "Mobile Branding" activity and also find other target segments which they can concentrate on to give immediate boost to the sales of the product, thus improving the financial position of the firm. This will also bring enough investors to the company.

M.S. Chandrashekar (✉)
Capgemini India Pvt. Ltd, Bangalore, India
e-mail: csmscs@gmail.com

G. Sharma
Brocade Communications, Bangalore, India
e-mail: gsharma13@gmail.com

B.P. Rangadhol
Altisource Business Solutions India, Bangalore, India
e-mail: basanth.rangadhol@altisource.com

A. Petkar
HSBC, Indian Institute of Management Kozhikode, Kozhikode, India
e-mail: Ashwin.petkar@gmail.com

M. Mookan
Indian Institute of Management Kozhikode, Kozhikode, India

A. Adhikari
Department of Marketing, Indian Institute of Management Kozhikode, Kozhikode, India
e-mail: Atanu.Adhikari@iimk.ac.in

Case Objectives

The case is structured to achieve the following learning objectives:

1. Understand how to strike balance between short-term opportunities and long-term goals and develop ways to earn smaller yet significant revenues critical for the firm's operations.
2. Help students appreciate the importance of being Market Orientated for a firm, especially when it wants to serve the B2B (industrial) market.
3. Help students identify the importance of segmentation of market and positioning of a product for focused marketing effort.
4. Learn how to effectively communicate the value of a B2B product to the targeted customers for the benefits and not just by the product specification.

Position in Course

This case has been developed for use in marketing management as well as marketing strategy courses and is appropriate for MBA, executive development programs and advanced undergraduate courses in international business and marketing. The case fits nicely in courses that deal with market strategy for small and medium enterprises and product positioning in emerging economies as well as in specialized modules focusing on international business.

Suggested Assignment Questions

Following are the major issues that GTPL founder Anjan needs to address to turnaround the financial position of the company and at the same time identify target segments for effective market strategy.

1. Is GTPL, an early start up in an emerging market, right in its approach towards being more Product Oriented and less Market Oriented?
2. Should Irrway™ be positioned in the mall segment for "Mobile Branding" activity to get a breakthrough in customer sales, but at the same time risking the dilution of the brand?
3. Suggest how GTPL should go about an effective Marketing strategy to have better market success. Also suggest whether "going green" is a viable branding strategy for Irrway™.

Suggested In-Class Discussion Approaches

To dramatize the challenges and to get the class engaged, the instructor could start by asking, "Do you believe GTPL followed the principles of market orientation while developing the product Irrway™?"

The instructor should proceed with the discussion on the assignment questions with an emphasis on the need to balance short term and long term strategies.

Some strategies that GTPL may consider and their pros and cons are discussed in subsequent sections.

Analysis

1. Is GTPL, an early start up in a growing market, right in its approach towards being more Product Oriented and less Market Oriented?

Pros:

- GTPL had done the initial market research on the evolving scenarios in the Electrical Vehicle (EV) space in India, growing trend of higher disposable income with the urban middle class in India, people ready to spend more on products that they feel esteemed to own. Based on the above data points, Anjan and GTPL believed that Irrway's true customer value will be easily seen in the urban centers and the product will be an immediate success.
- In case of a high end technology, normally customers are not able to articulate their exact needs, thus a basic product in the form of a prototype model is required for them to express their exact requirements. In this case, GTPL developed the product with core features and was flexible to provide accessories as per the requirements of each target segment. For e.g. providing golf kit holder on the product targeted at Golf courses segment.

Cons:

- Since GTPL wanted to sell the product in the B2B segment, a segment where prospective buyers do have a good idea about their requirements, it should have done some vendor and user research to effectively target a given segment. A good opportunity analysis and forecasting on the green personal mobile vehicle space would have allowed GTPL to focus on only those segments that it could satisfy both effectively and profitably.
- GTPL in its marketing communication could have focused more on the customer benefits and the solving the last mile connectivity issues that can be derived from the product Irrway.

2. Should Irrway™ be positioned in the mall segment for "Mobile Branding" activity to get a breakthrough in customer sales, but at the same time risking the dilution of the brand?

Suggestions

- Since Irrway was designed to have accessories specific to each target segment, the overall look and feel of the Irrway variant for the mall segment would certainly be different than look and feel of the Irrway variant that would be used in other segments such as the villas or gated communities and golf courses. Chances of Irrway getting over-exposed while being run as a "Mobile Branding" platform in a mall are less as the product has a specific role and look in each of the segments.
- Irrway as a product needs to build lot of awareness and positive impressions in the minds of prospective customers and positioning it in a mall for "Mobile Branding" is an excellent promotional opportunity to showcase it to the general public and generate buzz about it. Greendzine should be ready with pamphlets that contain information on core benefits of Irrway, being a green product and other promotional information.

3. Suggest how GTPL should go about an effective Marketing strategy to have better market success. Also suggest whether "going green" will be a viable branding strategy for Irrway™.

Suggestions

- GTPL should conduct surveys to develop the profile of an Irrway buyer and also identify target segments that can be served profitably.
- GTPL should be positioned in the target segment on the basis of product differentiation. Irrway can easily be differentiated among various products providing transportation. The points of differentiation from its closest competitor it holds are:
  (a) Ease of transportation, no energy needed in moving from one location to another.
  (b) Very much balanced, no training needed to use it.
  (c) Provision to carry basic goods such as bags, water bottles etc.
  (d) Safety to drive in dark with provisions of light and automatic sensing devices to detect obstacles in the way.
  (e) Easy re-charging.
  (f) Environmental friendly and a very sustainable product.
- GTPL can communicate the value of its product to the prospective customers by providing Irrway on rent for a reasonable price or for without any charges during the festive times so as to convince the customers about the utility and value-add provided by Irrway.

"Going green" will be a viable branding strategy for Irrway provided the product is communicated as a green product and many promotions and awareness campaigns are done to create the buzz around green. This will eventually allow GTPL to charge a premium price on Irrway as customers will be ready to pay a higher price for esteem.

What Happened

In order to find answers to the challenges that GTPL had been facing, it conducted a primary market research in the form of user and vendor survey along with an online survey on Green Awareness.

These surveys were conducted on fairly large samples. Below are the important conclusions derived from the survey results:

From the overall respondents of Green-awareness online survey,

- Over 53% felt that pollution due to vehicular traffic and other transports cause heavy environmental degradation.
- Over 78% are willing to buy green technologies product.
- Over 68% felt that greener technologies would solve global warming issues.
- Over 61% thought cost is important to adopt greener technologies.
- Over 65% felt the need to have a product like Irrway to commute short distances rather than walking.

The User and Vendor survey revealed the below information:

- Over 44% people liked Irrway because of it being a green product.
- Over 48% and 44% respondents found the utility of Irrway in Vilas/Apartments and IT parks respectively.
- Over 60% wanted to use Irrway to commute short distances than to walk.
- Over 50 and 27% had indicated that price and maintenance as a deciding factor to buy Irrway.
- Over 89% have preferred customization of the product Irrway for various features such as laptop holder etc.

Based on the above survey results and the response for the various demographics, psychographic and behavioral parameters in the survey questions, a typical customer profile of an Irrway buyer was created. The buyer profile would be as follows:

- Age between 10 and 65 years.
- Educated and concern for Green/Environmental issues.
- Higher income level—HNI category (high net worth individuals).
- Lifestyle should involve outdoor activities, visiting places and leisure sports like golf etc.

- Should be an innovator, early adopter, influencer with good self-conviction.
- Should seek good usage and benefits from products.
- Should be a person who is responsive to education campaigns and awareness programs.

Based on the above customer profile for the product Irrway, the below segments were chosen to be the most promising and profitable ones.

- Residential Gated Communities
- Golf Courses

Anjan Continued with Malls as Another Segment

A primary market research in the form of a face to face survey with retailers in various malls was done to gaze their responses to Irrway's potential as a mobile branding platform for their businesses inside malls.

The survey results of the mall retailers depicted the following points:

- Over 95% respondents liked the idea of Irrway as a tool for mobile branding and advertising.
- Over 86% respondents felt that Irrway as a mobile brand and advertisement platform will help them.
- Over 57% respondents had indicated that they would like to deploy Irrway as a branding and advertising tool in next 1–6 months.
- Over 52% respondents had indicated that they want to be among the early adopters to use mobile branding and advertising concept.

Based on the above, Irrway as a product was deployed in the mall retailers' space as a tool for mobile advertising and branding. In this segment, it was not seen as a green product and was positioned purely for the value that it was creating to the mall retailers.

Moreover, mall retailers had indicated that they were ready to place orders for Irrway within 1 week to next 6 months. This generated a good source of income for GTPL and improved its financial position.

The mall retailers had also shown interests in the various attachments that would be needed on Irrway ranging from advertising hoardings, accessory display stands and catalog hanging. With these attachments, the overall look and feel of the Irrway variant for the mall segment was certainly different than look and feel of the Irrway variant that was used in the Villas/Gated Communities and Golf courses. There was no case of over exposure of the Irrway as it had a specific role and look in each of the segments.

Teaching Note: Case 11: Citrus Ventures—Distressed Asset Specialist

Harsha C. Shastry, B.T. Lakshmipathi, Manohar, M.G. Srenath Rau, Pankaj Kumar Jatarya, Sachin M. Kamtikar, and Atanu Adhikari

Focus of the Case

Citrus acquired two distressed assets (both in real estate) in Bangalore and intended to complete the development, market the product and exit the projects at a profit. One of the projects was a residential project located off Sarjapur Road. The project involved development of 65 "row-houses" (which are villas connected to adjacent units by a common wall), marketing the unsold inventory and handing over the units to the end-user. This residential project is to be the focus of our study.

H.C. Shastry (✉)
Neev Capital, Bangalore, India
e-mail: harsha@neevcapital.in

B.T. Lakshmipathi
Global Class Room Pvt. Ltd, Bangalore, India
e-mail: lakshmipathibt@gmail.com

Manohar
Avani Software Education, Mangalore, India
e-mail: manohar.hello@gmail.com

M.G. Srenath Rau
AFS Logistics and Equipments, Chennai, India
e-mail: srenath.mg@gmail.com

P.K. Jatarya
ONGC MRPL, Bangalore, India
e-mail: Jatarya@mrpl.co.in

S.M. Kamtikar
Tech Mahindra, Pune, India
e-mail: sachinkamtikar@gmail.com

A. Adhikari
Department of Marketing, Indian Institute of Management Kozhikode, Kozhikode, India
e-mail: Atanu.Adhikari@iimk.ac.in

Marketing topics covered:

- Market segmentation and selection
- Demand and supply assessment
- Value offering and branding
- Satisfaction of various stake-holders
- Marketing strategy
- Marketing channels

Learning Objective

- Understanding of the business of Citrus Ventures from a marketing perspective applying frameworks learnt in class.
- Understanding nuances of various challenges faced by Citrus Ventures and come up with pertinent and practical solutions/workarounds for the challenges.

Topics of Analysis

- Market segmentation and ideal target segment for the project—a detailed study.
- Creation/enhancement of brand equity of Citrus Ventures in residential real estate space—a strategic approach.
- Quantification of benefits of appropriate marketing strategy—an evaluation.

Synopsis

Citrus is a distressed asset specialist, which takes over stalled projects and helps developers and bankers to complete execution and liquidate the asset. Citrus has taken over SpringVille at Harlur Road, Bangalore as a pilot project. The project is priced attractively in the market but has not seen great retail interest.

Analysis

- Analyze the value being provided by Citrus to the purchaser
- SWOT analysis of the business model being adopted by Citrus
- Market segment being targeted by the product
- Positioning of the product vis-à-vis the market
- Role of market intermediaries
- Product, price, place, promotion
- Financial analysis of the choice faced by Citrus

Teaching Note: Case 11: Citrus Ventures—Distressed Asset Specialist

Value Analysis

Average price paid by existing owners	8	INR Million
Average market price of equivalent assets	18	INR Million
Average market price of SpringVille assets	12	INR Million
Pending realization	70	INR Million
Total number of sold units	56.0	
Pending realization per unit	1.25	INR Million
Investment to date per unit	6.75	INR Million
If project is stuck potential recovery value to owners (at cost)	6.75	INR Million
Market price if completed	18	INR Million
Cost to be incurred to complete registration	1.25	INR Million
Value to owners if project is completed	16.75	INR Million
Difference in value in the two scenarios	10	INR Million
Cost to benefit factor	8.0	X

Citrus should communicate the following clearly to the existing owners:

- The recovery value of the property in the case the land is registered in the name of the owners and later sold on an as is where is basis is INR 6.75 million (they might have to sell at cost or less).
- The market value of the property if Citrus completes it is INR 18 million (on the basis of a 6600 per sq. ft. sales price—as per market comparables).
- The additional payment pending on average from each of the owners is INR 1.25 million.
- Hence, the additional value that Citrus is bringing into each unit of the project is INR 10 million.

SWOT Analysis

Strength	Weakness
Professional management team Strong network in Banking circles	Lower capital resources Negative connotation associated with distressed assets
Opportunity	**Threat**
Large market and industry size Generation of goodwill with end users and Bankers	Delays can cause damage to reputation Projects can require larger capital outlays than planned

Market Segment Analysis

- Positioning of SpringVille as a middle class offering might not be optimum.
- Based on the analysis of the market data for IT industry—the typical mid-level executives can afford units in the price range of INR 5–6 million only.
- Positioning the product as an affordable luxury/high-end development might be a good strategy.
- Senior—executives can better afford at the prices being offered.

Positioning

- Although the direct customer is the Developer and the Bank the final realization is dependent on the revenues from unit purchases.
- Goodwill with Developer and Bank can be generated indirectly through delivery of project to unit purchases.
- End-users are more susceptible to emotional decisions rather than business men and bankers who can analyze value brought to the table by Citrus in a detached manner.
- Positioning to the public and intermediaries (brokers) should not be as a redeveloper/distressed asset specialist—it should be restricted to the corporate world.
- Rebranding (including renaming the project) might go a long way in reducing the negative connotations associated with the project.

Market Intermediaries

- Instead of targeting 500 brokers it might pay off to go with a dozen brokers who have been educated on the value of the project to the new purchasers and better informed.
- Incentivize brokers through fixed price plus model (whatever excess they earn is to their benefit).
- Given that the best ambassador for any project is a satisfied end-user, register and complete at least 2 units in the project to end users who can occupy the premises in the short term.

4P'S

Product: The product being offered is superior to the competitors offering since the specifications are all similar to each other (POS) but Citrus is offering to register divided share in land which gives better flexibility to owners.

Price: The price being offered by Citrus is 33% below market price. This sends out a negative signal to the end purchaser regarding the quality of the asset. Since sales are slow irrespective of price, either sales can be put on hold till progress is achieved in the development or can be pushed at a higher price.

Place: The project is conveniently located in close proximity to both Electronics City and ORR-Sarjapur Road and thus is best suited to be marketed to the captive audience working in the region.

Promotion: Since the number of units to be sold is only nine and the target customers are high-end customers, a mix of intermediaries (for investors) and direct selling in high end retail locations such as UB City (for end-users) as well as promotional activities in large campuses such as Infosys might be beneficial to the project.

Financial Analysis

Vinod's predicament is a choosing the right point in the trade-off between rate of sales and sales price of the project. Change in Sales Price has the following impact on profitability (PAT)

Change in Price from INR 12 million (%)	−10	−5	0	5	10
Profitability in INR Million	16	21	26	31	36

Any further reduction in sales price will make the project un-tenable to Citrus. Also since it has been proved beyond doubt that there is significant value to the end customer even at the price point Citrus is currently offering. Hence the reason for the slow sales is not high sales price but softer aspects associated with the project.

If Vinod infuses capital to take the project to certain level of completion over the next 3 months and hence is able to achieve a better performance in terms of rate of sales and average sales price the trade-off could be as below:

Infusion of capital	Non-infusion of capital	
Infused capital—20 million	Infused capital—0	
Rate of sales achieved—1 per month	Rate of sales achieved—0.5 per month	
Sales price achieved—5000 per sq. ft.	Sales price achieved—4500 per sq. ft.	
Total sales realization—INR 122 million	Total sales realization—INR 109 million	
Difference in price	13	INR Million
Duration for realization	9.0	Months
Investment	20	INR Million
Returns	95%	IRR

What Actually Transpired

Vinod and his management team took up a series of measures in order to successfully complete the project. Chiefly these were as follows:

- Added more projects to reduce administrative and other overheads on this project (from INR 0.8 million per month reduced to INR 0.3 million per month over 6 months).
- Bought back 3 units from old customers who were most vocal and opposed to any further collection by Citrus—this was done through an agreement to purchase in the next 3–6 months (minimal upfront payment of INR 0.5 million).
- These units which were purchased at cost, INR 8 million, were again marketed at INR 12 million to the public.

Since there was no end-user selling in the project the communication from old customers to new customers stopped and aided remediation of project image.

- Citrus swapped units in the project with vendors in lieu of monetary payments—hence without infusing working capital the project construction resumed.
- Vendors also felt comforted since work resumed and some small payments were made from new sales and new collection.

The project was successfully completed with the last few units selling at market price landing a handsome profit for Citrus Ventures which has from there went on to acquire several distressed assets.